CW01660160

A Historical Report

The Rastafari Movement In England

Norman W Adams (Jah Blue)

This book was first published in 2002
by **GWA Works**

ISBN: 0-9543025-0-8

Typeset, designed and printed
by R.U.Z. Comprint
London, England.

This book is dedicated to the
ancient Patriarchs, Matriarchs and Martyrs of Rastafari,
those and them that
TROD THROUGH GREAT TRIBULATION.
Also to my dear Mother, a Sistren of Rastafari.

To Jerome
One Perfect Rastafari
Love
[illegible]
24/8/07

"Weaklings never start, and Cowards die on the way."
a Rastafarian proverb

"An individual who does not utilise his energy to better his condition, is like one who dismembers himself. To depend only on things produced by others, does not bring complete happiness. To enjoy the fruits of one's toil, encourages and strengthens the creative spirit, sustains one's pride and contributes in a most tangible way to security and Happiness."

Emperor Haile Selassie I
Addis Ababa 1949 Exposition

The Author

I was born Norman Washington Adams on 23rd April 1949 in Kingston, Jamaica. My parents were political activists and my maternal grandmother was a member of Marcus Garvey's Universal Negro Improvement Association (UNIA); she was active in the women's auxiliary.

I grew up on Hill Avenue, Tower Hill, Kingston 11, and attended Half-way Tree School until 1962 when I moved on to Tarrant Senior School off Molynes Road, Kingston. In January 1963, I left Jamaica with my Father to join my Mother in England. I was nearly fourteen years of age.

Tower Hill community where I grew up was predominately working class, with a few well to do families in the area. Kingston in the 50s was quite peaceful, comparing to the late 70s and 80s. Political tribalism was unknown then, and there were no street gangs, even though this phenomenon had started to develop from the late 60s. From 1958-60 there was an upsurge of Rasta activities in Kingston of which I was well aware and had witnessed at first hand.

The Reverend Claudius Henry established an organisation, The 7th Emmanuel Brethren, followed by The African Reformed Church with headquarters at 78 Rosalie Avenue, about 200 yards from where I lived at Hill Avenue, Kingston 11. The area was buzzing with the activities of the Reverend's organisation. I, along with some of my friends, would try to go around to the HQ without our parents knowing. I had first hand account of events as they unfolded in the hills of St. Catherine, Jamaica. I had no idea how these events would influence me in my later years, or that I would identify with these people.
After I left Jamaica I had no further contact with the Rastafari Movement until 1968 when I went to a blues

dance in Ladbroke Grove. At first glance I was surprised, I had no idea that the Brethren were in London. However by 1969 I had contact with Bro. Asento Foxe and Shaggy Berry and that was the beginning of my involvement in the Rastafarian Movement.

Today, I am a Rasta activist, writer and lecturer on the history of the Movement. At the University of Cape Coast in Ghana I presented a paper at PANAFEST '94, titled "Uniting the African Family".
I am also a qualified Community and Youth worker and helped to establish several youth projects in England, my most successful being the Simba Community Project in Shepherds Bush, London W12. I am also an active member of the EWF Inc.

Contents

1. Introduction
2. Brief History of Jamaica
3. Brief History of the Movement
4. Early History in England
5. The Jamaican Working Committee
6. Britain in the Late Sixties
7. The Universal Black People's Improvement Organisation (UBIO) 1969-71
8. Revitalisation of the People's Democratic Movement (PDM), Political Wing of the Rastafari Movement
9. Delegation to Jamaica 1972
10. Background to the Ethiopian World Federation, Inc.
11. Ethiopian World Federation, Inc. Local 33
12. Delegation to New York and Jamaica 1973
13. Charter 15 - Twelve Tribes of Israel/Delegation Returned to England
14. The Ethiopian Orthodox Church
15. Establishment of the Ethiopian Orthodox Church in Britain
16. Growth of the Movement in Britain
17. International Recognition 1980s
18. Repatriation
19. Brief Summary of the Movement
20. Characteristics of Rastafari and its Organisations
21. Mission to Africa Report 1961
22. Chronology of the Movement

1. Introduction

Since the emergence of the Rastafarian Community in England, there have been many booklets and articles written about the Movement and its development. However most of these have been damaging, inaccurate and misleading. In the early 1970s when the Movement started to become more popular amongst young black people, many local and some national press did their utmost best to try and discredit it.

They portrayed the Movement as a lunatic "cultgroup" whose members were involved in all kind of criminal activities and whose intent was to control organised crime in Britain, hence the description "Black Mafia" was used by some journalists to describe the Movement. No attempt was made to put across the serious fundamental aspect of the Movement, one of whose contribution has been to raise the consciousness of millions of Black people all over the world and whose ultimate objective is repatriation to Ethiopia Africa. *"We cannot give up a continent for an island"* is a popular Rastafarian saying.

To date Earnest Cashmore's book *"Rastaman: The Rastafarian Movement in England"*, 1979 is still regarded by some as the first serious attempt to examine the history of the Movement in this country. He was helped in his research by Claudius Haughton, a Rastafarian Brethren who was the President of the Ethiopian World Federation, Inc. Local 33, Unit (1) in Birmingham 1974.

During this period I myself was one of the four international officers for the said organisation residing in this country. Since Cashmore's book, two other booklets have been published which many Rastafarian Brethren and Sistren have observed or acknowledged for their recommendations on behalf of the Movement. These are:

"Rastafarians in Jamaica and Britain" (Notes and Report No. 10) by the Catholic Commission for Racial Justice, 1982, and *"Rastafarianism in Greater London"*, published by the Greater London Council in 1982. Both these documents however have had to rely on Cashmore's book for some of their references. My reason, therefore, for writing this book is to provide a primary source of material for future sociologists, educationalists, Black Youth and Rastafarians who genuinely wish to know how the early Rastafarian community developed in Britain.

I have also taken the opportunity to include an unedited report from the Governor of Jamaica, K.W. Blackburn, to the Secretary of State for the Colonies, Alan Lennox Boyd, MP. This will give an insight into the British Government's attitude and policies toward the Rastafari Movement from the 50s onwards (C.S.O. Ref: CSP99 Jamaica Dispatch No. 637. (1959)).

I hope this book serves as proof and gives an insight into the high level of organisational activities within the Movement. As a participant within the Movement in England since the late 1960s, and as an executive officer of the Ethiopian World Federation, it was an essential part of my duties to submit regular reports to the executive body. These reports have been quite useful in helping me to accomplish this project. Other sources of evidence have been Brethren and Sistren who were active since the late 1950s, 60s and 70s, some of whom now live in Jamaica and Africa. Others, still residing in Britain, are now founder members of various other Rastafarian organisations such as The Rastafarian Advisory Service, Rastafari Universal Zion, Twelve Tribes of Israel and Rasta International, and Local 33 Church Triumphant Housing Welfare Co-operative.

In Cashmore's book I am one of two people credited with the birth of the Movement in England. I am referred to in this book by the name Gabriel Adams (Wold); this is incorrect as my Rastafari name is Gabre-Wold Adams.

I will also humbly submit that I am not the founder of the Movement in England, nor was I a part of the group that started here in the 50s. I believe this honour would be more in keeping with the names of other brethren such as Ascento Foxe, Roy Prince, Bro.Tull and Bro. Shaggy.

Special mention should be made of Ascento "Emmanuel" Foxe who has been instrumental in helping to develop the Movement in Britain and who provided me with most of the information and material which cover the period between the late 50s early 60s.

Now that the Movement has achieved global significance and national importance in the Black community, the need for a factual account on how the Movement developed in England cannot be over emphasised. I hope this book will go a long way in fulfilling this need. I would like to express my sincere love and appreciation to all the Brethren and Sistren who have encouraged me to do this project, many of whose names I have not mentioned in this book, but to whom I am deeply indebted for their support and encouragement.

I would also like to thank Delroy Thompson, Ras Keambiroiro, Ras Lenroy, Bongo Deshi, Ras Tekla (E Wright and Sista Dee for their efforts on this book, i.e. typing and all the associated word processing, as without their help, this project would not have been completed.

Acknowledgement
Photo by - Rev. Z.E Yohannes, Levy and Lance Watson.

2. Brief History of Jamaica

To understand the history of the Rastafari Movement, we have to start with the history of Jamaica.

Jamaica is the largest island in the British West Indies at 4,411 square miles. It is isolated from the rest of the English speaking islands in the West Indies; St Kitts, the nearest, is over 800 miles away and Trinidad is over a 1,000 miles to the east. Cuba to the north is the nearest island and is only 90 miles away on the north coast of Negril.

The island is 150 miles from east to west and 50 miles from north to south with the Blue Mountain, the highest point at 7,600 feet in the eastern side of the island. The population of two and a half million is 78% African Black, 1% white, 1% Chinese, 2% East Indian and 18% Mixed race. More than a quarter of the population lives in Kingston, the capital where the main port, industrial, administrative and cultural centres are situated.

The island was discovered by Christopher Columbus on his second journey to the new world, in 1494. By 1509 the Spaniards began to settle in Jamaica and eight years later the first Africans were brought to the island, in 1517. From that time onwards, the people of African origin began to play a significant role in the growth and development of the island.

There was no gold in Jamaica to satisfy the Spaniards so the island was used as a base to supply the Spanish with men, horses, food and arms for the conquest of Cuba and the American mainland. Goats and cattle were imported into the island and they multiplied quickly, roaming all over the island. Each year there would be a big hunt, resulting in skins and hides being exported to the Spanish American mainland.

The use of Africans as cowboys, hunters and herdsmen by the Spanish, resulted in the Africans living a semi-free existence, thus becoming familiar with the interior of the island. In 1589 the African population was increased when 155 Angolan slaves were sold at a public auction in the island.

The island of Jamaica as a Spanish colony was poor and badly governed. There were some scattered settlements on the island, but only one town, Villa de la Vega known as Spanish Town. The island was always under threat from the constant raids of the Dutch, French, English and Portuguese pirates. The Governor at the time, Fernando Melgarego de Cordova (1597-1606), would ask for support from Puerto Rico and Cuba to help fight off the pirates' raid on the island.

By 1640 the peace loving Arawak Indians had witnessed the destruction of their culture and society. However, the Africans were much tougher and they began to assert themselves on the island. By the time the English took over, the population of Jamaica was a Spanish African one with a mixture of Arawak Indian blood.

On the 10th of May 1655 the English landed on the island. Admiral Penn and General Venables arrived with 38 ships and about 800 men. The Spanish, seeing they were no match for the English invader, abandoned the island and went over to Cuba, with their families and some of their slaves. However, some of the Africans chose not to stay with their Spanish masters and went off into the Jamaican hills and wild interior. They were to become the original Maroon. No one is sure of the derivation of the name Maroon but it is rooted in the history of Jamaica.

The conquest of Jamaica by the English was not complete. At once there was a Spanish resistance movement led by

Don Cristobal Arnaldo de Ysassi. De Ysassi, a Spanish Jamaican, went into the hills and tried to win the support of the slaves who were now living in the Jamaican hills. A few Africans did remain loyal to the Spanish cause but a large number led by a leader called Juan Lubdo, later known as Juan de Bolas, in the hills of Clarendon were undecided; no one knew if they would support the English or Spanish.

Within the next five years de Ysassi waged a constant guerrilla warfare against the English, with the help of some Africans in the hills, but he could never count on their complete support. He was fearful that they could also take side with the English and lead them to his camp. When Jamaica fell into the hands of the English, Cromwell issued a proclamation on land grants for settlers who transported themselves to Jamaica. This brought many other settlers to the island.

The English were quick to realise the value of an African auxiliary, and launched a determined effort to woo them from the Spaniards with false promises of instant freedom and land. De Ysassi also tried the same policy to win the support of the Africans but he was unsuccessful. He was also at a disadvantage in that he had to wait on orders from the king of Spain before confirmation.

On the 23rd September 1659, Oliver Cromwell, the Lord Protector died, and Charles II was restored to the throne. These events caused some insecurity amongst the English forces in Jamaica. De Ysassi used the opportunity to attack the English as ferociously as he could, but this failed. By the end of February 1660 Juan de Bolas, who had the largest African following, was given land by the English and the privileges of free men. De Bolas was also appointed colonel of a black regiment. De Ysassi, realising what had happened, knew that his day on the island was finished.

On the 9th May 1660 de Ysassi left the island with his men and went over to Cuba. This marked the end of the Spanish resistance in Jamaica.

With de Ysassi leaving the island, the English Lieutenant-Governor, Sir Charles Littleton in 1663 made a renewed offer of freedom and land to Africans in the hills of Jamaica, if they surrendered. The Maroons scorned this offer, they had taken their freedom and his offer meant nothing to them. The English patience grew exhausted and they decided to wipe out the menace of the Maroons once and for all. The instrument for this project was Juan de Bolas. However, on his first mission against some of his old comrades he was caught in an ambush; his forces were cut to pieces and de Bolas killed himself. The death and the defeat of Juan de Bolas increased the confidence of the Maroons. It also spelt an end to an era in the early history of Jamaica.

The Spanish threat to Jamaica now ended with the departure of de Ysassi. Military government came to an end and civil government established. Jamaica was now a British colony. The pattern of settlement was small at first but new settlers came from Bermuda, New England and Barbados.

Sugar became one of the world's foremost commodities and sugar estates of great proportions for the cultivation of sugar cane grew up on the island. The production of sugar on the large estates needed a large amount of workers. Europeans could not take easily to this kind of hard work needed and so the English began to import large amounts of Africans to Jamaica as slaves.

The people who came to Jamaica as slaves were mainly from West Africa; they were Eboes and Yourbas from Nigeria, Mandingoes from the South Coast of Sierra Leone, Koromantees (Akim, Asante and Fanti people from

Ghana) some people from Congo and Angola, but of all the people who came, it was the Koromamtees from Ghana (the Gold Coast) who stood out.

The Koromantees, according to the planters, were strong, virile and fierce, and were not the kind of people to accept slavery. Along with other brave spirits from the groups they were always looking for the opportunity to escape. There were many individual escapes but there was a big slave outbreak in 1684 and the second in 1686. Some of the slaves were captured but many of them eluded capture and went into the hills to later join the Maroons. The original Maroons had settled in the east and the north of the island but most of the runaways chose to settled in Clarendon, among the old haunts of Juan de Bolas. It was from amongst that small group that a young Koromantee named Cudjoe Accompong was to emerge from obscurity. With Cudjoe as their leader the Clarendon runaways defied all efforts to subdue them. Over the next 30 years he became a tough and aggressive guerrilla fighter, and they too became known as Maroons, like the earlier runaways. The Maroons were a constant thorn in the side of the British settlers and the country was in a state of war until 1739 when the British sued for peace. The treaty was signed jointly by Captain Sadler, Colonel Guthrie and Chief Cudjoe.

Jamaica in the 17th and 18th centuries was the world's largest producer of sugar. Under the Treaty of Utrecht* of 1713, Britain took over from France, through the Spanish Asiento Charter, the contract to distribute slaves to the Spanish colonies for 30 years. Jamaica was a distribution centre for slaves until the trade became illegal in 1807. It is estimated that over 1 million slaves were brought to the island but many were re-exported to other parts of the Caribbean and North America.

*Footnote: Utrecht is in Holland (Editor)

By 1755 the white Jamaicans were outnumbered at about fifteen to one by their slaves and were in constant fear that Jamaica would become another Haiti. Through this French colony the entire French army were wiped out and the first black republic in the Caribbean was established. The slave revolts in the French colonies were inspired by the French revolution. The Jamaican planters were fortunate in that this did not happen in Jamaica but the fear was always there.

The people who came from West Africa as slaves soon lost their language and customs as they were put together with other tribes in work gangs and could only communicate in the English that they picked up. However this did not stop them organising amongst themselves. Every leader or conspirator of a rebellion was a Koromantee and the tribe from West Africa turned out some very colourful leaders. Cudjoe, Nanny, Quacao, Three Finger Jack, Tacky Quashie, Sam Sharp, Paul Bogle and Blackwell all raised rebellions which were always put down with torture and death. Tacky, rather than face death at the hands of the British, committed suicide.

In 1834 after a bitter struggle between the British parliament and the Jamaican Planters Assembly, slavery was abolished. The fear of a slave revolt was the reason why the Jamaican planters resisted emancipation.

Emancipation

What difference did emancipation make in the life of the former slaves? They had no land and no provision was made for them. They had no legal property of their own; the small hut and garden they had on the master's plantation was not their own anymore. It was in the planters' interest to provide health and medical welfare for the slaves but now, no such consideration was relevant anymore.

Many slaves were evicted, a few remained in their cottage huts but the planters forced them off, hoping they would be dependant on the wages to make them stay. But most of the slaves could not be persuaded to work on the plantations anymore. Many went to the hills and squatted on crown land.

The Emancipation Act of 1833 saw the decline of the Jamaican plantation system, which had dominated the economy for over a century. After the Napoleonic wars, depression hit Jamaica very hard. Growing competition from Cuba, Puerto Rico and Europe for the beet sugar meant Jamaica never regained her former position on the world sugar market. Also, after emancipation the shortage of labour helped to compound the situation, and within the next half a century, the British started to import Chinese and Indian indentured labourers onto the island.

In 1846 Britain had a free trade policy, which took away Jamaican tariff advantage. Many planters went bankrupt and left the island, some of their land was later sold to the ex-slaves. The large number of plantations dwindled from over five hundred to just under seventy at the start of the twentieth century.

By the early 1900 the black population had doubled and the small supply of land for the hillside farming was soon exhausted. There was a large surplus of labour which could not be absorbed inside Jamaica and large numbers left the island to seek work elsewhere. The Panama Canal, banana growing in Costa Rica and Honduras, and the sugar cultivation in Cuba were all projects in which thousands of Jamaicans went to seek employment.

By 1924 over 100,000 West Indians, most of them Jamaicans, went to America. Some did contract farm work and many served in the last two world wars in the United States Armed Forces.

In 1938 the centenary for emancipation was not a public celebration and there was nothing to mark the events, but a wave of strikes and riots rocked the whole of the West Indies. In Jamaica this led to mass labour movements and reinforced the nationalist movement for independence. These movements accumulated in 1943 with a popular constitution which gave the people of Jamaica universal adult suffrage. The background to this social and economic turmoil was different from the situation created by the declaration of emancipation in 1838.

By 1938 there was a large brown-skinned middle class in Jamaica, the result of the promiscuous relationships between the white slave master and the black slave women. They were born into the legal status of slaves, but their fathers bought their freedom and they were educated and financially provided for. These mulattos themselves owned over 50,000 slaves before emancipation, and their descendants represented the hard core of the middle class of 1938. This also included some Asian and Chinese who were prominent as merchants and traders. The middle class was strongly influenced by the British upper class and went to great lengths to assimilate British characteristics. Although there was no legal discrimination against the black man or people of colour, there was a "white bias" built into the society which puts the African at a disadvantage. European standards of beauty were set by the white upper class although a black man with money and education was socially acceptable to a degree.

The women would straighten their hair and bleach their skin. Some black men went to extreme lengths to adopt British attributes such as exaggerated Oxford accents and mannerism and ultra British names for their children. Since difference of skin colour and hair texture were socially significant, a black man with money would always try to marry a woman of more European appearance than his own in order to raise the colour of his family and to socially advance.

The desire to marry brown or white has left a large number of well-educated black spinsters on the island who had no opportunity to marry men of their own social class.
While the upper and middle classes were very busy building an imitation of Britain, the Jamaican black massive lived in another world, a world with its roots in Africa, slavery and deprivation.

Since emancipation, little has happened to change the social and psychological habits connected to such a past. Emancipation had made over 350,000 black slaves into citizens of Jamaica, but apart from this, they had no property, no education, limited skills and had to fend for themselves. They did not even have the institution of family life. From 1836 to 1938 not much had changed in the conditions of the black working class in Jamaica, except that the population had tripled to over one million.

Political Development

Although the black masses were the majority, they were kept down with little trouble during seventy years of crown colony government. The blacks and mulattos out numbered the whites on the legislative council but never acted as agents of the black massive. They were black Englishmen and they themselves could not see the concept of black nationalism preached by Marcus Garvey from the 1920s.

In 1938 serious strikes and riots broke out at the Tate and Lyle sugar estate in the western end of Jamaica. Cane fields were set alight, some company officials were assaulted, four people were killed and hundreds arrested. It was against this background that Alexander Bustamante came on the political scene in Jamaica. The son of an Irish planter, he was born in Jamaica in 1844 and travelled as a young man to Spain where he lived, as well as to Cuba and sometimes the U.S before he returned to Jamaica in 1932. Although the 1938 riots lasted over a month, Bustamante appeared to figure largely at the scene of every incident until he was arrested and charged with sedition and unlawful assembly, but his arrest only made him more popular among the masses.

After Bustamante was arrested it was his cousin Norman Manley, K.C and one of Jamaica's greatest lawyers who came to his defence. At Manley's intervention, Bustamante was later released and the pair started working together. They visited trouble spots all over the island and helped to negotiate on the behalf of the strikers and their employers. However, rivalry developed between Manley and Bustamante. Manley then went on to establish The People's National Party (P.N.P) and Bustamante set up the Jamaica Labour Party (J.L.P).

The 1944 constitution was the first step towards Jamaica's independence, and gave universal suffrage to the Jamaican people in the first election. Bustamante won with twenty-three out of thirty-two seats leaving the P.N.P with four, and five independent in the house of representatives. Jamaica had now acquired representative, but not yet full government. After two defeats, Manley realised that he had to get to grips with his party. Inside the P.N.P there were quarters known as the Four H's, the two Hill brothers Hart and Henry. They were very active in the party and the trade unions. The Four H's were seen to be too militant, and they were publicly expelled on the charge of bringing communist propaganda into the party and the trade union. Manley, with a new image as "the father of the nation and man of destiny", won the 1955 election with a comfortable victory. In 1957, major changes were made to the constitution and Manley, formerly known as the Chief Minister, now became the first Prime Minster of an all elected government with full internal power. Over the next twenty years Jamaican politics was dominated by Manley and Bustamante.

By the 1960s the outward trappings and progress of Jamaica were phenomenal in the field of economic development with few resources besides human labour. Jamaica had answered the challenge by making rapid economic progression and the foundation for this development was the discovery of bauxite and the development of tourism. There were also signs that the colour-class stratification was breaking down, owing to the democratic process over the past twenty years. Kingston looked like any modern capital with its banks and gleaming government buildings. However, there was still another side to this developing country.

Marcus Garvey

Marcus Mosiah Garvey was born in 1887 in St Ann, Jamaica. He was the youngest of eleven children and was the first Black man to preach Black nationalism to Black people in the western world.

As a young man, after leaving Jamaica, he travelled to South and Central America where he saw, at first hand, the condition the Black people were under in those countries. He visited Honduras, Nicaragua, Venezuela and Panama where he was able to observe the conditions under which his countrymen were living. Many had come to seek employment in building the Panama Canal. He tried to organise the Black workers in those countries but had little success.

Marcus later left Panama and went back to Jamaica, then on to London. In London he spent time further educating himself and it was there that he read *'Up from Slavery'* by

Booker T. Washington and decided that he would work for the liberation and upliftment of his people.

Marcus Garvey returned to Jamaica in 1914 and within weeks he established the *Universal Negro Improvement Association (U.N.I.A).* The aim of the organisation was to unite all Black people of the world into one great body. The motto of the organisation was *'One God, One Aim, One Destiny!'* The organisation, as well as having aims for the Black people of the world, also had plans for the Black people of Jamaica. It proposed the establishment of an educational and industrial College for Jamaican youths along the lines of the Tuskegee Institute which was founded by Booker T. Washington.

This was accepted by some prominent citizens including the Mayor of Kingston. But most of the ruling class in Jamaica were opposed to it, and he came in for a lot of criticism from them. Garvey said, after they rejected his plans,

"Men and women as Black as I, and even more so, had believed themselves white under the West Indian order of society. I was simply an impossible man to use openly the term 'Negro', yet everyone beneath his breath was calling the blackman 'nigger'. I had to decide whether to please my friends and be one of the 'black-whites' of Jamaica, and be reasonably prosperous, or come out openly and help improve and protect the integrity of the Black millions and suffer. I decided to do the latter.

In 1916 Garvey went to America. He started his programme, and visited some of the Black leaders, but to his surprise he found out that they were mere opportunists, who were living off the poor Black people. Within a few months he had established the headquarters of the U.N.I.A in Harlem, New York, from where it spread and became a mass movement. Within a couple of years, and ultimately the UNIA became the largest Black movement ever, by and for Black people.

Marcus preached that the Blackman should not consider himself inferior to the whiteman, that he should take pride in his race and turn his back on following western culture, turning, instead, to his own African culture, otherwise he could not discover his true self.

He preached *'Africa for the Africans'*, those at home and those abroad. Garvey was working for the creation of a new state in Africa to receive the Black people of the west who wanted to return. He also founded the 'Black Star Line', a shipping line with the intention of transporting Black people there.

In his 'Philosophy and Opinions' he wrote: *"I asked myself, Where is the Blackman's government? Where is his King and Kingdom? Where is his President, his ambassadors, his army, his navy, his men of big affairs? I could not find them, and then I declared, I will help to make them."*

Marcus Garvey worked hard to establish the Black Star Line shipping company, but it was infiltrated and sabotaged, leading, subsequently, to Garvey being sent to prison for fraud. In 1927 Garvey was freed from prison, deported from the United States and returned to Jamaica. Soon after arriving in Jamaica, Garvey founded the Peoples Political Party, the following year, but his doctrine did not please the white and brown Jamaicans who wanted to build Jamaica as a small England. He gained one seat on the City Council, but was later briefly jailed for contempt of court.

After this, Garvey left Jamaica for England, where he died in 1940. Before he left Jamaica he told his followers to *"Look to Africa when a Black King shall be crowned, for the day of deliverance is near."*

The year 1930 saw the coronation of His Imperial Majesty Emperor Haile Selassie I, and many of Garvey's followers, after consulting the Bible, accepted that this was the Black King that he had spoken about. Several preachers then took to the streets of Jamaica and began to preach the doctrine that Haile Selassie I is the Living God.

During the development of the Movement the basic concepts were that Haile Selassie I is God, repatriation to Africa is a must, and that the Black race is the Children of Israel. The early Rastafarians turned their back on western culture and worked instead on developing their African culture. They were proud and stuck to a Mosaic morality.

The Rastafari believe that ganja is the sacred herb described in the book of Genesis, which unites them spiritually with God, and gives them wisdom and health and strength. Nothing can persuade the Rastafari that ganja is bad, and anyone who attempts to try to stop them from using it is seen as the devil.

It was quite common in the early days, that many Rastafari who were brought to court for possession of ganja, defended themselves and would tell the judge that they did not accept the jurisdiction of a temporal court and could only be tried in heaven. Because of the non-conformity of the Movement, many brethren were victimised in every possible way by society. Because of this hostility towards the Movement, the Rastas withdrew themselves from society rather than play an active part within it to change it. They do not consider themselves Jamaican but citizens of Ethiopia/Africa.

In 1955, Emperor Haile Selassie I made a land grant in Shashamane to the Black people of the west. It was during this time that migration fever was in the air, as Britain had opened its doors to the people in the West Indies in order to recruit cheap labour in the rebuilding of her war-damaged economy.

A sociologist during that time, doing a survey in Jamaica on the unemployment condition of the country, found that all the households who were surveyed assumed he was compiling a list of all the people who wanted to return to Africa.

In 1959 a man named Reverend Claudius Henry, R.B (Repairer of the Breach) returned from the USA to his home in Jamaica. He began to preach repatriation to Africa before the end of that year. He printed thousands of tickets, giving the 5th of October as the date for repatriation. Many Rastafarians and ordinary Jamaicans sold their houses and all their possessions in preparation for the journey home to Africa, but repatriation did not happen.

A few months later, Henry's son, Ronald arrived from the US with the objective to take over the Jamaican government. With a small band of uniformed brethren, he went into the hills of St. Catherine, in a Castro style operation. He was captured a few days later, but not before the death of two British soldiers and three Rastafari brethren. The police raided Henry's HQ and found dynamite, detonators and two letters addressed to Castro, asking him for his support in capturing Jamaica.

Henry was charged with treason and sedition and was sentenced to ten years. His son was captured and hanged along with two of his comrades. The whole incident brought panic and world-wide attention to the Movement. In the Jamaican ruling circle, the Movement was previously the object of amused scorn, now it was regarded for the first time as serious threat to the island's security.

The whole incident brought a wave of hostility against the already persecuted Rastafari Brethren. Some leaders of the Movement contacted the Principal of the University College of the West Indies to put across their views to the general public. The report, which was completed in one month by messrs. Smith, Augier and Nettleford, pointed out to the public that *"The great majority of Rastafari brethren are peaceful citizens who do not believe in violence. Nevertheless, since the movement is heterogeneous and includes all types, its members range from complete pacifists at one end to criminals, the mentally deranged and revolutionaries at the other."*

On the subject of Communist infiltration, a possibility at the time, which struck terror in the Jamaican establishment, the report had these warnings:

"We have no evidence that Ras Tafarians, as a group, are being manipulated by non-Rastafarians with violent beliefs, such as Communists. Rastafari doctrine is radical in the broad sense that it is against oppression of the black men, much of which derives from the existing structure. But it has no links with Marxism, either of analysis or of prognosis. The movement has been infiltrated by a number of criminals, but these people are essentially individualist and have little ideological influence. For the Jamaican leftist, the violent part of the Rastafarian spectrum is a gift; capitalist, bourgeoisie and proletariat can be directly translated into white, brown and black. Revolution becomes Redemption with Repatriation as the issue provoking bloodshed... In so far as this political philosophy employs the ideology of Rastafari racism, its spread throughout the bulk of the population is assured unless government takes positive steps to meet the legitimate needs of the lower classes, including the Rastafari group. The choice before Jamaica is that between social reform which is planned, peaceful and rapid on the one hand, or changes of a different sort.

It is certain that Jamaican society cannot continue in its present form. Since economic development presumes social stability, this means that any successful development depends on an intelligent programme of social reform. The recent spread of Rastafari doctrines among educated middle class youth is largely due to the appeals of ganja and Marxism, but this spread will surely continue so long as Jamaican society fails to provide the young with significant ideals of social justice for which to strive, and opportunities for their achievement. Regarding the structure of the Movement, the report observes that: *Its sheer complexity makes manipulation by troublemakers exceedingly easy. Those interested in the ganja traffic, whether at home or abroad, find a serviceable instrument in the Rastafari brethren... those merely interested in defrauding people and pursuing personal gain find a ready market in the Rastafari movement. It is perfectly clear that all these... types of manipulators are active among the brethren. Only their mutual competition has prevented a major upheaval so far. How long this will continue remains to be seen. In the dense slum areas (of Kingston) the prevailing doctrine and ideology is now Rastafari."*

The report went on to recommend that immediate attention should be given to the Rastafari needs. This ranged from education, improved housing facilities and employment, to an end to police brutality and victimisation.

The Prime Minister accepted the report's recommendations and sent a mission to Africa to examine the possibility of repatriation. The mission left for Africa on 4th April 1961. It is against this background that we will look at he growth of the Movement in England.

3. Brief History of the Movement

The birth of the Rastafarian Movement in Jamaica, as we know it today, can be traced to the Coronation of His Imperial Majesty, Emperor Haile Selassie I of Ethiopia.

In Ethiopia-Africa and for Black people all over the world it was the dawn of a new era. Regarding the event Dr David Talbot writes, in 'Silver Jubilee of Haile Selassie I', *"Sunday November 2nd 1930, nature seemed to have agreed that the weather should be appropriately fine. On Coronation day at 7 am, the Emperor and Empress-elect followed by members of the Imperial family, dignitaries and others, arrived at the Church of St George's Cathedral. This followed a night of prayer and thanksgiving. His Imperial Majesty took His seat upon the twin throne, Her Imperial Majesty to His right. As part of the solemn and majestic ceremony the Emperor read Psalm 101 aloud. His Holiness Abuna Kyrihlos, the Archbishop, exhorted the people to be loyal and obedient to the Emperor, the Elect of God. A part of the exhortation read: 'Ye nobles and Chief of the army, ye soldiers and people of Ethiopia; Look ye upon the Emperor Haile Selassie I, descended from the dynasty of Menelik I, who was born of King Solomon and the Queen of Sheba, a dynasty perpetuated without interruption from that time to King Sahla Selassie and to our time...'"*

For many Black people in Jamaica this was seen as no ordinary event. Some began to consult their Bible to find out if this was the fulfilment of Marcus Garvey's prophecy before he left Jamaica. For Garvey had said: "Look to Africa where a King shall be crowned for the day of deliverance is near." The Emperor, apart from having the legal title, King of Kings, Lord of Lords, Conquering Lion of the tribe of Judah, the Elect of God, also, according to Ethiopian tradition, traced His ancestry to the union of King Solomon and the Queen of Sheba. Several individuals, after confirmation with the Bible, took to the streets in

Kingston, Jamaica and began to preach of Haile Selassie I as God, the returned Messiah, the Christ of this dispensation.

The following passages from the Bible were used to prove the Emperor's divinity:
Revelation 5:5 *And one of the elders said unto me, Weep not, behold the Lion of the Tribe of Judah, the Root of David, hath prevailed to open the book and to loose the seven seals thereof.* Revelation 19:16: *And He hath on His vesture and on his thigh a name written, King of kings and Lord of lords.* Revelation 22:16: *I am the root and the offspring of David, the bright and morning star.* Psalm 87:4: *Behold Philistia and Tyre, with Ethiopia this man was born there.* In general, many passages in the Bible were used to support the claim of the Emperor's divinity, including: Isaiah chapter 43; Malachi chapter 1:14; Revelation 5, 17, 19 and 22 and Psalm 9, 18, 48, 68 and 76. In 1941 when the Emperor returned triumphant from exile, further proof was found in Revelation 17:14 *They shall make war with the Lamb, and the Lamb shall overcome them; for He is the Lord of lords and King of kings and they that are with Him are called, and chosen, and faithful.*

The early advocates of the doctrine of Ras Tafari (Haile Selassie I former name) although small at first, began to grow. The invasion of Ethiopia by Italy and the establishment of the Ethiopian World Federation, Inc. all helped to increase world attention on Ethiopia, and the doctrine of Ras Tafari took firm roots in the island of Jamaica. The doctrine was developed by several individuals, including Leonard P. Howell, Joseph M Hibbert and Archibald Dunkley. However, Leonard Howell, along with his deputy, Robert Hinds were the most dynamic of the early preachers. Other brethren also made their contribution to the Movement such as Almont Reid, Vernon Davis, Paul Earlington and Ferdinand Ricketts.

The Movement today is noted for its religious outlook but it was also a response to political and socio-economic conditions. Basically they all preached the same things but with variations according to the personality involved. All except Archibald Dunkley claimed the divinity of Haile Selassie. Dunkley, who had read the Bible for two and a half years, said he did not believe Haile Selassie was God Himself, but a messenger. However, while they, the early preachers, might differ in their interpretation of the Bible, the basic concepts were:

1. Haile Selassie I is the true and living God
2. Black people are the original Israelites
3. Ethiopia-Africa is the Garden of Eden/Zion
4. Repatriation back to Ethiopia-Africa is a must
5. Africa for the Africans, those at home and abroad
6. The Pope represents the devil
7. The western world is Babylon.

Essentially, all Rastafarians read their Bible, but are quick to admit there are omissions and wrong interpretations. Around the biblical theme, the Brethren also preach Black consciousness and the need for social and economic reform. It is interesting to note that in 1934 when the first confrontation between the government and the Ras Tafarian community in Jamaica took place, Leonard Howell and Robert Hinds were charged for sedition. Joseph Hibbert and Archibald Dunkley were also arrested and imprisoned in what was a systematic attempt to destroy the Movement in its early infancy.

The Movement faced continuous and increased persecution from the government and the upper and middle class Jamaicans, who regarded the Rastafarians as social outcasts. They were discriminated against in all walks of life and were constantly attacked by the media. The Movement, however, continued to grow and took firm roots among the working class people of Jamaica.

In the 50s, migration to Britain by many Jamaicans assumed major proportions. How the Movement developed in its new environment and provided an international platform for its members is what we shall examine in the following chapters of this book.

4. Early History in England

During the 50s many Jamaicans migrated to England. Amongst them were members of the Ras Tafari community. This was in response to the British government policy of the day; they were recruiting Black people from the Commonwealth to help rebuild the economy after the last war. For many Black people within the British Empire at the time, this seemed only natural. Fifteen years earlier they had responded with enthusiasm to help defend the democratic ideals of the West.

The opportunity to improve their social and economic development was seized with open arms and thousands came, followed by their families. It was a great shock and bewilderment for many to find out they were not welcome by the indigenous English community. Although some islands, like Barbados, had their nationals recruited directly by London Transport into a job, the Jamaicans had to find their own fares, which meant selling their possessions such as their home and land, etc. There was no institution to process and resettle the newcomers. They had to survive in their new home against a background of racism, discrimination and prejudice in every form. In 1958 racial violence spilled out into the streets of Notting Hill, west London, and parts of the Midlands in Britain.

Today, Notting Hill is famous for the Carnival that is held annually. It is also significant because this was the area where our beloved prophet Marcus Mosiah Garvey spent his last years. He was based at number 2 Beaumont Crescent, W14, from where he distributed his publication called The Black Man. The scene of major race riots in the late 50s, it is also the birth place of the Ras Tafari Movement in England.

In 1958, "a group of bearded and rather conspicuously dressed young Black men were noted in the Brixton

Market area. Several local informants confirmed that they were Rastafarians." (Sheila Patterson's *"Dark Strangers"* 1963, p. 354). During this time a small group of Brethren were meeting in the Notting Hill area. Some came from North London and Brixton. Amongst the group who were meeting at 40 Powis Garden, Powis Square, W11 were Roy Prince, Ascento Foxe, Clifford Gully, Keith Shaggy Berry, Earl Luke, Desmond Christie (Brother Ruddy), Nicholas McCoy (George Painter), Keith Miller (Brother Pilot) and Brother Tull. Most of the Brethren were committed Rastafarians from Jamaica while others had sympathised deeply with the Movement in Jamaica.

Ascento Foxe, Roy Prince and Brother Tull were members of the Ethiopian World Federation, Inc., Local 37 in Jamaica.[1] This was one of eleven locals which had been established in Jamaica in 1955 when Miss Maymie Richardson came to the island on behalf of the organisation's HQ in New York.

Footnote: (1) Ras Sam Brown was the President and Martino Planno the General Secretary of Local 37 during this time in Jamaica.

5. The Jamaican Working Committee

(Official Contact with Ethiopian Government.)

In 1960 the Brethren in London, after meeting as a group for two years, were authorised by the executive of the Ethiopian World Federation, Inc., Local 37 in Jamaica, to function in London as a sub-local of Local 37.

On 10th March, 1960 the Brethren had their first official interview at the Imperial Ethiopian Embassy, Princes Gate, London. One of their requests was for a Royal Charter of the Ethiopian World Federation Inc. The Counsellor at the Embassy said he could not commit his government officially without consultation, but expressed his sympathy with, and his interest in, the Movement. It was the first official contact between members of the Rastafarian community and the Imperial Ethiopian Government, and a dialogue was established.

Subsequently, in June 1960, the Cultural Attache from the Ethiopian Embassy visited the sub-local and had further talks. It was during this visit by the Cultural Attache that the Brethren were given the name "The Jamaican Working Committee."

After the Cultural Attache's visit, two members of the Committee met the Ambassador, Endelkachew Makonnen[1] at the Ethiopian Embassy. They explained their aims and objectives, which were sympathetically received. The Ambassador said he would undertake the responsibility to become the mediator between Ethiopia and the Rastafarian Brethren in London, and would give all help possible.

Footnote: (1) Endelkachew Makonnen, the last Prime Minister of Ethiopia (1974-75) died in Ethiopian Revolution, Bloody Saturday.

He also stated he would put the Brethren in contact with one of the dignitaries of the Ethiopian Orthodox Church, whom he felt would be the right person to tackle some of their problems. At the end of the discussion, the brethren were told they should prepare a written report on the Movement, so this could be studied by His Majesty when he, the Ambassador, returned to Ethiopia. These developments were very significant when one considers that until then, not even in Jamaica did anyone within the Movement have any contact with the Imperial Ethiopian Government. It was during this time that the University College of the West Indies carried out the first official report on the Rastafarian community in Jamaica.

This report was at the request of the Rastafari Brethren who felt that both the government and the upper class people in Jamaica should be given the opportunity to gain some insight into the Rastafarian community and its doctrine.

This also came about because of the activities of the Reverend Claudius Henry's organisation which caused the Rastafarian community to experience one of its worst confrontation with the government of Jamaica.

As a result of this report, the famous mission to Africa took place the following year, 1961 (see report in a later chapter). Local 37 in Jamaica was aware of these developments and was informed about the contacts that had been made with the Ethiopian authorities. The findings of the Jamaica Working Committee, Sub-local 37, were published in a booklet entitled *"Rastafarians Past and Present."* They are as follows:

The Rastafarians had no voice in the legislature of Jamaica and must accept the need for representation. They could not advance the aims of the Movement or reach the masses until they took practical steps to form a political wing of the Movement. A new and practical attitude of mind was needed amongst the members of the Movement. They must be made to realise the vital necessity of accepting political responsibility and a reunification of their social activities and general approach towards the community.

These findings were not accepted by some of the members of the executive of the Ethiopian World Federation Inc. Local 37 in Jamaica. However, after some deliberation, the brethren in London, who were now in contact with the Imperial Ethiopian Government, took the decision to form a political wing of the Movement, with the eight point plan for progress, which are as follows:

1. Hitherto, Rastafarians throughout the history have never sought direct representation for members of the Movement. Now we have realised that our aims cannot be achieved without some form of official representation. We wish to have, and to be able to nominate our own candidates for election without fear of persecution which we have suffered in the past and with due regard to the fundamental laws of human rights.

2. Repatriation to Africa for those Jamaican nationals who so desire it, with a realistic approach to this migration, and the realisation that this can only be achieved at government level. Pioneer schemes must be organised to meet the practical needs of the country of the intended migrant. The ultimate right to the nationality of the African country chosen should be conferred on the intending migrant as and when he or she qualifies for it by virtue of their residence and merit of their contribution to that country.

3. Establishment of the Ethiopian Orthodox Church in Jamaica as the recognised and official Church for members of the Rastafarian Movement. At present there is no official representative of the Ethiopian Orthodox

Church in Jamaica, and members of our Movement who are deeply and sincerely religious have to worship in groups established as camps led by an elder who is looked upon as a chaplain. These exponents of the faith and scriptures, who observed certain days in common with the Ethiopian Orthodox Church, are liable to develop individual lines with ideological interpretations of their own, and personality cults and divisions amongst members of different groups have arisen as a result of these different concepts being preached.

Another problem which the establishment of the Ethiopian Orthodox Church would help in solving is that of the undesirable elements who look like Rastafarian brethren but who are, in fact, not true sincere members of the Movement, but are using it as a cover for their activities and bringing disrepute onto the Movement.

In order to achieve this constitutionally, we have taken the decision to form a political wing of the Ras Tafarian Movement which will be known as the People's Democratic Movement, in the effort to achieve the aim of Ras Tafarian representation in the legislature of Jamaica, through an orderly constitutional channel.

4. Freedom of choice and equal opportunity in employment within properly enforced conditions of work, and protection against unemployment. At present the Rastafarian who, because of his religious belief grows his hair and beard, has little hope of employment as there is almost universal discrimination against him by other members of the community.

Some Rastafarians have been forced to cut their hair and beard in order to get employment. To date no form of legislation protects those who wish to preserve their deep religious beliefs, and work. Consequently many

Rastafarian are unemployed through no wish of their own, and the Movement is branded as being largely composed of people who do not wish to work. This serious discrimination has caused great hardship and the inevitable lowering of standards of living of members of the Movement.

5. Co-operative Development in commerce and industry should be assisted as one of the answers to objective 4. At present many Rastafarians, spurned by the community in general, have to develop art and craft and trade amongst themselves (into groups) in order to eke out an existence. They have formed themselves into small groups and co-operatives, which need encouragement and expansion especially with regards to co-operatives in order to raise the social and commercial standard of the Rastafarian community. This is a practical step which has already had its foundation prepared and now need official recognition and assistance.

6. Education facilities are extremely limited under the present system, two thirds of the population of Jamaica get no more than an elementary education. Many are forced to leave school before they complete their education through sheer economic necessity of having to go out and work to help the family budget. More emphasis should be placed on technical training, and the teaching system should be revised. The history of Africa should be taught in schools instead of the intensive study of European history, which is of less direct interest to the people of Jamaica.

7. Health and Housing, the serious understanding of the already inadequate hospitals should receive immediate attention, and the training of doctors and nursing staff increase, with reasonable conditions and incentive given to trained staff. The present medical facilities do not meet

the requirement and must be revised and improved if the people's health and hygiene are to progress.

8. Under the present system, the desperate need for housing cannot be met. Conditions are unspeakably bad, with shanty towns which have sprung up on many parts of crown land and private property. Some overall planning is essential if the dangerous gap between the haves and the have-nots is to be bridged. The need is urgent as conditions of the underprivileged people in Jamaica is appaling and apparently without hope of improvement.

It would be foolish to ignore the risk of letting such conditions prevail to nourish the seed of revolution. Conditions which are so indifferent to the suffering and misfortunes of a large number of people surely cannot be the will of God for man. These eight objectives demonstrate a new realistic approach in the development of the Movement and shows the emergence of the Rastafarian ideals with practical propositions to meet the need of the people of Jamaica in general. The Rastafarians now know they must be more practical and realistic, and they realise that in order to achieve official recognition, the basic essentials are:

(1) Unification within the Movement
(2) A different approach to the community
(3) A constitutional approach to ensure the rights of the individual.

As the aims and objectives clearly show, the early Rastafarian Brethren in England took a political stance, and their programme was geared towards the development of the Movement in Jamaica. However, no real effort was made to propagate the doctrine to the wider Black community in England, at the time, and this policy continued until the late sixties.

From the first meeting at the Ethiopian Embassy, the Rastafari brethren in London had discussed the various problems that had beset the Movement with the Ambassador. He had fulfilled his promise, and on his return to Ethiopia, he put the brethren in contact with Abba Habte Mariam Workneh, personal chaplain to His Majesty, and communication had begun. In 1963 he met four of the brethren at the Ethiopian Embassy and further discussions took place.

Ascento Foxe, who was present, said they the Brethren were advised that they should return to Jamaica and help organise the Movement into a more institutional body. They were also promised financial assistance, which was confirmed in a letter from Abba Worknen dated 10th September 1960. The suggestions to return to Jamaica and organise the Movement was not accepted by all the brethren at the time, and only helped to create more internal problems among them.

Desmond Christie (Bro Ruddy) was one of the Brethren who had no intention of returning to Jamaica and, in 1967 he went to live in Ethiopia, on the official land grant in Shashamane, largely through his own efforts. He was among the first Rastafarian from England to migrate to Ethiopia and later helped to secure a tractor to work the land, with financial assistance from the Brothers in North London, notably Ras JB, Bro. Lambie, Bro. Rennie, and Bro. Bunny (L. Wright). Some of these brethren now live in Jamaica. Desmond Christie now lives in Kenya with his Ethiopian wife and children. He has lived there since 1976, following the Ethiopian revolution in 1974.

While these Brethren did not make any impact on the wider community at the time, their influence, even in the early days, had begun to manifest itself within the Black community in West London. It is certain they were involved in confronting the race riots that had spread to

Notting Hill Gate from the Midlands during the summer of 1958. They were also instrumental in the fight against "Rachmanism" at the time.

Peter Rachman, a Polish immigrant who came to England at the end of the Second World War, was one of the biggest racketeers in Britain during the late fifties. Between 1954-59 he owned over two hundred residential properties in Notting Hill and other parts of West London. He made a vast fortune exploiting the Black community who were hard-pressed to find accommodation in those days. One of his henchmen was the late Michael de Freitas (Michael X) who was executed in Trinidad in 1975 for the murder of Gale Ann Benson. It was the Rastafari brethren who confronted Rachman and finally exposed him. He died in 1962 of a heart attack.

The decision by the Brethren in London to form a political wing of the Movement was not accepted by many of the leading brethren in Jamaica, and this helped to strain the relationship on both sides. In April 1961 the Mission to Africa, which was sponsored by the Prime Minister of Jamaica, the late Mr Norman Washington Manley, spent one week in London. They were met by the brethren and various talks took place, on what kind of assistance could be given on the Mission's return from Africa. In June 1961 the Prime Minister of Jamaica, Mr Norman Manley came to London for official talks with the Government of Britain.The brethren sent a letter to him asking for an interview and a report on the Mission to Africa.

Development within the Movement, dealing with repatriation, did not get off the ground in Jamaica, after the Mission had returned from Africa; failure to organise and study the logistics of such a programme gave the Government ample reason to quietly shelve the whole idea. Working as the People's Democratic Movement, political wing of the Rastafari Movement, the brethren made contacts with various African Embassies and Nationalist groups based in London. Letters of introduction and the booklet titled "Rastafarians Past and Present", were sent to each group, who welcomed the change from the non-political stance previously adopted by the Brethren.

However this caused serious division among the brethren themselves. Some of them could not see any reason why they should return to Jamaica, when geographically Ethiopia / Africa was nearer to England.

This contention was never resolved and the result was that by the end of the sixties, most of the brethren from North London stopped attending the gatherings in West London on a regular basis. However this did not stop them from propagating the doctrine in their respective communities in informal gatherings or in their homes.

Although the Brethren made little impact on the wider Black communities in the sixties, they were not without commitment. As early as 1962 four Brethren, on their second attempt, left London and drove through to France and Spain to Morocco to finally reach Ethiopia. The group, led by Cliffton Macloud*, had an audience with His Majesty and was given the opportunity to reside in Ethiopia if they so desired. According to Ascento Foxe the brethren had a deliberate policy to maintain a low profile, so as to educate themselves for their future role within the Movement, and to explore and examine the spiritual and ideological concepts of the doctrine.

*Footnote: Cliffton Macloud (alias Judgement) went back to reside in Jamaica in the early 70s.

6. Britain in the Late Sixties

By the end of the Sixties the Black Communities in Britain were beginning to adjust themselves to life in their new environment. The Immigration Act was introduced under the Conservative Government in 1962 and finally endorsed by the Labour Party in 1964 when they produced their White Paper on "Immigration Control". This policy was to effectively restrict the entry of Afro-Caribbean people from the West Indies coming to England. The racial violence that erupted in America during the mid-sixties evoked deep sympathies among the Black people in the U.K. "Black Power", the slogan which emerged from the Civil Rights Movement in the US, echoed the sentiments of Black people all over the world.

In 1967 when Stokely Carmichael came to Britain, he launched the Black Power movement in this country. He was born in Trinidad and grew up in New York, where his parents migrated to when he was young. After his tour of some of the Black communities, he made a speech at the Round House, Chalk Farm, London. As one of the activists within the civil rights cause in America he was well received by Britain's Black intelligentsia who gathered to hear him define Black Power as *"the coming together of Black people to fight for their liberation 'by any means necessary.'"* Carmichael's speech was considered dangerous by the British establishment and shortly after he left the country, the Home Secretary for the Labour Government, Roy Jenkins, announced in the House of Commons that Carmichael would not be allowed into the country again. "Having considered a report on this man's recent activities I have decided that his presence here is not conducive to the public good," he said.

The next few months saw a new wave of militancy from various Black power leaders in Britain. During this period

Roy Sawh and Michael de Freitas (Michael X) became the focus of attention by the media for their activities. Both were charged with inciting people to racial hatred under Section 14 of the Race Relations Act, after making what was called inflammatory speeches to their audiences. Of the two, Michael X was the more controversial figure and he was sentenced to one year imprisonment. Roy Sawh was fined.

Michael de Freitas was born in Trinidad 1933. He was one of many young men who came to Britain during the fifties with the hope of improving his personal development. By the early sixties he was well known in the Notting Hill ghetto, as a hustler. His reputation amongst the Notting Hill Black community was well known during his association with Peter Rachman in the late 50s. After a chance meeting in London with Malcolm X, the Black activist of America's racial conflict during the 60s, he was soon identified as Michael X, the leader of the Black Power Movement in England.

In 1968 when Michael X had finished his imprisonment for the race offence, Britain was in the grip of racial tension. A Large influx of Asians holding British passports were leaving East Africa under the country's policy of "Africanisation". Enoch Powell, a member of the Conservative party, was dismissed a few months earlier from the Conservative Shadow Cabinet for his speech in Birmingham on immigration. It was against this background that the Universal Black People's Improvement Organisation (UBIO) was to emerge in the early part of 1969 in Notting Hill.

7. The Universal Black People's Improvement Organisation (UBIO) 1969-71

By the end of the 1960s a new generation of Black youth had emerged in England. Most had come to join their parents or relatives during the late 1950s and early 60s from the West Indies. Some also had brief contact with the education system, and by the time they went out on the open job market they had experienced all forms of racism and discrimination which were blatantly open in British society during those times.

In 1969 an organisation emerged in Notting Hill which might have seemed insignificant at the time, but its impact on the development of the Rastafarian Movement in England was very unique and fundamental to this day.

The Universal Black People's Improvement Organisation (UBIO) was officially established on 9 April 1969 and was based at 225 Westbourne Park Road, London W11. Originally a neighbourhood association, it was taken over by the local Black Activists in the community. The office was an old shop which was converted during weekdays, and general meetings were held every Thursday evening at the Co-op Hall on All Saints Rd, W11 (now known as the Front Line Ladbroke Grove). This organ also operated a Youth Wing and published a monthly journal called "UJAMAA".

The more dynamic part of the leadership of this organisation comprised of two Rastafari Brethren, the Chairman Ascento Foxe (Brother Pinto) and Keith Berry (Brother Shaggy) from Brixton. The Secretary was Anthony Mohipp* a professional Lawyer from Guyana. The rest of the executive was made up of Black intellectuals and Garvey-ites.

*Footnote: Anthony Mohipp is now a High Court Judge in Guyana.

At the general meeting which was held every Thursday at the Co-op Hall, the audience was a who's who in the Black community. At the time many leading Black Activists of the 60s could be seen amongst the crowd in those days, to name but a few, Darcus Howe, Frank Crichlow, Rhoden and many others. The only white face amongst the crowd was Lord Anthony Gifford, QC, although only a few people knew who he really was. The meeting was open to the general public, and embraced a wide audience in those days. Meetings would open with the Rastafari National Anthem: "Ethiopia The Land of our Fathers, the Land where our Jah loves to be".

After the anthem the meeting began and many issues of the day were debated. The atmosphere was intensely political, and the legacy of Black Powerism, which was strong in the late 60s, was reflected in the meetings. In 1969 when a black power mutiny by a part of the Army in Trinidad was aborted, the meetings at the Co-op Hall helped to keep the Black communities informed on events in Trinidad and went on to mobilise support for a demonstration against American involvement in Trinidad's internal affairs.

The office at Westbourne Park Grove which served as an advice centre did the best it could in giving support and legal advice to the Black community whenever necessary. It was a tremendous effort on the part of those people who undertook this work because we must remember this was a voluntary organisation.

From the initial beginning the UBIO reflected a wide spectrum of views amongst the Black intelligencia and activists who attended the meetings in those days. But at the height of this organ's brief history, there was a split in the leadership. By the end of 1970 all the radicals and pro-Marxist elements had been ousted, leaving the leadership of UBIO firmly under Ascento "Pinto" Foxe and Keith "Shaggy" Berry. From this point onwards the UBIO was completely eclipsed by Rastafarians.

The Youth Wing of this organisation played an important part in these developments, for it was amongst these youths that the Rastafari Movement would find new adherents to the faith, to catapult it into the 70s and onwards in Britain.

UBIO Youth Club

After the changes that occurred within the organisation, much more emphasis was placed on the youth programme. The UBIO Youth Club had a full and varied programme and began to develop more openly within the concept of Rastafari doctrine. Rasta doctrine was propagated within the programme of the Club, with an emphasis on education. The membership of the Club grew quite rapidly and became quite influential amongst many youths in the surrounding Black community. Most of the membership came from West London and the Brent area, but there was a strong following from the Brixton area, such as Phillip Taylor (aka Frank-I-Jah or Ras Binghi), Frederick Smith (aka Fred-I-Jah) and Brother Tilly who now resides in Jamaica.

In West London were Sister Beverley Byrea (Wolette Madhin), Peter Letang, Larry Thompson, Winston Hibbert, and the two volunteer Youth Leaders, Basil Jarvis and Norman Adams, the author, also called Gabre-Wold Adams or Jah Blue, from the Brent area. There was also Maxim Anderson, Errol Powell, Sister Wonder and Junior Downer. Also amongst the membership of this Youth Club was the late Slim Smith, one of Jamaica's leading Reggae vocalist at the time. He died in mysterious circumstances in Jamaica, 1973. Another member was Claudius Massop, architect of the Peace truce between warring political gangs in Western Kingston, Jamaica in 1978. He was killed by police on 5 February, 1979 in Jamaica. His wife, who now resides in Jamaica, was also a member of the Youth Club.

Although the club was independent in its approach it did have official recognition from the then Inner London Education Authority (ILEA) and therefore did have access to some facilities available through the Youth Service. The Area Youth Officer of Kensington and Chelsea at the time, Mr Ian Durnford, visited the Club on many occasions, but was unable to persuade the membership to his argument of integration.

Although the UBIO had a brief history, it played a fundamental role in helping to develop the social and political awareness of many Black youths who came to the meetings. Today some are qualified people working in various areas of the Social Services Agencies. Others have become influential members of the Rastafarian community in England and Jamaica. As an organisation the UBIO was quite progressive in its heyday. Article (8) of its aims and objectives expressed the need for Afro-Caribbean history to be taught in schools. This was quite unique as the organisation itself came under question for using the term "Black-People". Then it was considered more appropriate by some people to use the word "coloured", as they found the word "Black" offensive.

Under the leadership of Ascento Foxe (Bro. Pinto) and Bro. Shaggy (Keith Berry) and Leroy Williams, Managing Director of the Youth Club, The UBIO Youth Club was able to develop along Rastafarian traditions. While on the surface the Club functioned on a conventional basis with a Football and Netball team, there was an intensive Cultural Class which dealt with the history of Ethiopia and

Rastafari. When the UBIO gave its first interview to Time Out Magazine in the early part of January 1971, the members were already making plans to dissolve the organ and to identify themselves positively with Rastafari.

This was due largely to the fact that Foxe and Berry as older members of the Movement were able to educate the younger Brethren and Sistren into the concept of Rastafari. Also, most of the Youth Club members at the time were of Jamaican birth and some, like myself, were already exposed to Rastafari in our early years in Jamaica.

The knowledge that equipped the young Brethren and Sistren for entry into the Rastafari livity was not only about the divinity of Haile Selassie I, but also the ancient history of Africa / Ethiopia.

Ever since the Black man was taken away from Ethiopia / Africa, European historians have carefully hidden the achievements of the Black race and its contribution to humanity. By researching our history we came to realise that our ancestors not only contributed towards human development, but laid the foundation for civilisation itself.

The Greeks, in their early writings, deified Black people, who appeared as their gods in Greek history. Heroditus and the early Greek historians all bear testimony to these facts.

Diodorus Siculus, a first century B.C. world historian, says: *"The Ethiopians say they were the first men that were ever in the world, and that to prove this they have clear demonstration, for, they say, they are native of the country and not strangers that came to settle there."*

"It is most probable that those who inhabit the south were the first living men that sprang out of the earth. For being that the

heat of the sun had first exhaled the moisture of the earth and in the first production of all things, influence it with a quickening virtue. They say that it is rational to conclude that those places nearest the sun should have been the parents of all living creatures."

"The Ethiopians likewise say that the Egyptians are a colony hewn from them, and that Egypt was made out of the mud and slime of Ethiopia, meaning that the rich soil brought down by the Nile. They further declared, according to this ancient writing, that "Egyptians got their laws, their customs, their burial rites, their statues and their system of writing from Ethiopia."

Stephen of Byzantium wrote, *"Ethiopia was the first established country on earth, and the people were the first who introduced worship of gods and who enacted laws."*

The young Brethren and Sistren, by re-educating themselves, were made aware that their ancestors gave to the world civilisation and therefore, they should not be ashamed at being Black. This history and knowledge were expounded by the prophet Marcus Garvey and were the main themes which he preached to the Black people during the 20s and 30s in the U.S.A and the Caribbean.

One of the main policy of the U.B.I.O was that the Organ supported all of the struggle that was taking place in the southern part of Africa by staging demonstrations as well as giving economic support.

In October 1970 the UBIO had acquired new premises, at 356 Portobello Rd, W10. Although this was more adequate for space, the building was earmarked to be demolished in the next 5 years for future council housing in the area. The ground floor of this building was used as the main office, the two rooms on the first floor were converted into the meeting hall and the second floor was used as a library and rest-room. From this building the UBIO was dissolved in 1971 and the members began to function under the banner of the People's Democratic Movement, the political wing of the Rastafarian Movement. This was due to the efforts of Pinto Foxe and Shaggy Berry who were functioning in this organisation in the mid 60s.

According to Maxim Anderson, 1986 Cultural Development Officer of the Simba Community Project, London W12, and an earlier member of the UBIO Youth Club: "The UBIO made a tremendous impact on our lives as young people and raised a whole generation of youth consciousness."

Britain in the Early Seventies

"The future of Black People in Britain is of crucial importance to race relation. The second generation of Black People may be less patient and perhaps, more militant in seeking their rights than their parents have been. They will expect equal treatment with their white contemporaries, and unless they get this treatment, the seed of racial conflict may be sown." (Jerry Okoro) "Black in Britain", Africa Magazine No. 9 May 1972.

In the early seventies, there was an already growing concern about Black youth in Britain. The few who had left school with qualifications were forced to take menial jobs. Many white employers were unprepared to give Black workers status over white staff. At the same time many black youths were experiencing police harassment in the form of "SUS", which meant they would be stopped at random by the police and charged on suspicion to commit some kind of felony. Unemployment and discrimination in housing led many Black youths to "squatting" (living in unoccupied houses).

Immigration was also one of the major issues in British politics with right wing organisations like the British Movement and the National Front openly advocating repatriation of Black people in Britain to their countries of birth. The echoes of British politician Mr Enoch Powell's famous 1968 speech on immigration, when he said he foresaw a bloody black/white confrontation in Britain in the near future, still lingered on.

8. Revitalisation of the People's Democratic Movement (PDM), Political Wing of the Rastafari Movement

In March 1971 the UBIO was phased out and the People's Democratic Movement revitalised. The aims and objective of this organisation were based on the Constitution of the Ethiopian World Federation, Inc. A monthly Newsletter was published called "The Rastafarian Cry." The mood of this organ however was quite different from its predecessor. The emphasis of the PDM was for youths to support a political wing of the Movement.

The executive of the PDM was comprised of those young brethren and sistren who were members of the UBIO Youth Club. Although most were Jamaican born, youths from other Caribbean Islands began to identify themselves with the Movement by this time. On the new premises at 356 Portobello Rd, W10 a general meeting was held on a regular basis. On Sundays some of the brethren with their families would attend the building for devotional exercise. This involved Bible reading and chanting, and was the preparatory stages for the development of the Ethiopian Orthodox Church.

In 1970 the Ethiopian Orthodox Church was officially established in Jamaica, by Archimandrite Abba Laike Mariam Mandefro, Head Administrator of the Ethiopian Orthodox Church in the United States of America and the West Indies. On his third visit to the island in August 1971, Abba Mandefro conducted the religious service of thanksgiving at the Holy Trinity Cathedral in Kingston to mark Jamaica's ninth Anniversary of Independence. Assisting the Archimandrite in the service were Rev. Eglon Evans of Guyana and Rev. Gilbert Anscot, Deacon of the Ethiopian Church, Jamaica. Present on this occasion were His Grace, the Most Rev. Samuel Carter, S.J., Archbishop of Kingston, the Rt. Rev. Cyril Swaby, Anglican Bishop of Jamaica, and the Governor General, Sir Clifford Campbell and members of the Rastafarian Community.

The Archimandrite, Abba Mandefro, read a message from His Holiness Abuna Theophilus, Head of the Ethiopian Orthodox Church in Ethiopia. Abba Mandefro urged the establishment of cultural exchanges between Jamaica and Ethiopia which he said would not be too difficult bearing in mind the many similarities between the peoples of both countries.

Sir Clifford Campbell also spoke. He said that Rastafarians in Jamaica were seeking an identity and the establishment of the Ethiopian Orthodox Church would go a long way in assisting them in that direction.

These events in Jamaica were observed quite closely by the Brethren and members of the PDM and it was decided that a delegation should visit Jamaica and bring the membership up-to-date on these recent developments.

The strong political theme advocated by the PDM has been the main input from A Foxe and some of the elder brethren in England, who had come to that conclusion based on their fact finding report in 1960. In particular, that in order for the Movement to fully respond to the needs of its members, it must accept some form of political responsibility.

This idea was not new, for from its early inception there was always a minority within the Rastafarian Movement who saw the need for it to address itself to social and political reform.

In the 1961-62 general election in Jamaica, Sam Brown, a Rastafarian, campaigned as a candidate under the banner of the Black Man Party. However, the general appeal which the PDM made to Black youths was that they should educate themselves in various skills and return to the Caribbean. In terms of the Movement in Jamaica it was decided that there could be no repatriation without representation, in the Parliament of Jamaica.

9. Delegation to Jamaica 1972

On Thursday 27 April, 1972, two members of the PDM executive left England for a six-week visit to Jamaica. They were Ascento Foxe (Pinto) and Norman Adams (Jah Blue). In Jamaica the Brethren were warmly received by the Rastafarian Community, who were quite pleased to know the Movement was developing in England. During their stay in the island, they attended various gatherings and reasoning sessions, and were introduced to many Brethren all over the island.

While the delegation was in Jamaica the Archimandrite, Abba Mandefro, visited the island at the official invitation of the Prime Minister of Jamaica, Mr Michael Manley. The presence of the delegation from London was drawn to his attention and a meeting was arranged for the Brethren to meet him.

On Saturday 20 May 1972 the delegation from London met Archimandrite Abba L Mandefro. The meeting took place at the Ethiopian Orthodox Church Rectory, Penrith Road, Kingston 14. the Archimandrite was given a full report on the Movement in England and the brethren's desire to have an official branch of the Ethiopian World Federation, Inc. and the Ethiopian Orthodox Church in England. After the discussion the two Brethren were baptised by the Archimandrite and given their baptismal name, Ascento "Emmanuel" Foxe and Norman "Gabre-Wold" Adams.

Abba Mandefro also said that on his return to America he would inform Mr George E Bryan, the International President of the Ethiopian World Federation, Inc., of the delegation's activities in London and they would receive an official charter of the EWF, Inc. The delegation was also given copies of the Ethiopian Orthodox Church liturgy, which would help in developing the church in London, and documents authorising the collection of funds for the building of the Ethiopian Orthodox Church in Jamaica.

The following day the delegation attended an Ethiopian Orthodox Church service which was then held at the Ebeneezer Church in Tivoli Gardens, Western Kingston.

During their brief stay on the island the delegation were instrumental in establishing a Youth Club in Western Kingston (Salt Lane) at the request of the youth in that community. On their visit on 18 May 1972 to the Youth Development Agency, based at Handover Street in Kingston, the delegation met Paul Miller the Parliamentary Secretary for Youth and Community Development. He expressed his deep appreciation for this venture which the Brethren had undertaken in such a short time. The Club was registered as the Haile Selassie I Youth Club.

On the delegation's return to London the membership of the PDM was given a full report on developments in Jamaica. The visit was a positive step by the Brethren and it gave them fresh impetus on which to build. It could also be said to be the turning point in the relationship between the Rastafarian Community in England and Jamaica. In Jamaica there was now a general awareness that there was a growing Rastafarian community in England, something that was not known previously on any large scale in Jamaica.

In terms of achievement, the mission by the delegation was a complete success. Fresh contact had been made with various groups and individuals within the Rastafarian Community. But most fundamental was the fact that for the first time the Rastafarian Community in London was identified within the mainstream of Rasta activities in Jamaica, which was dominated by the development of the Ethiopian Orthodox Church during the early seventies.

The visit to Jamaica also meant the final chapter in the life span of the People's Democratic Movement (political wing of the Rastafarian Movement). After communication began with Mr George E Bryan, the International President of the Ethiopian World Federation, Inc., the PDM was dissolved and a Steering Committee of the EWF, Inc. was formed. This functioned for the next few months until the Brethren received their charter on 25th August 1972 from the EWF Inc. Headquarters in New York (USA).

10. Background to the Ethiopian World Federation, Inc. (E.W.F)

In October 1935, when Italy launched a blatant act of aggression against Ethiopia, it generated a considerable amount of public outrage and sympathy among the African-American community. Enraged by Italy's assault on the world's last bastion of Black power, they began to make contributions to various organisations raising funds for the Ethiopian cause.

From the very outbreak of the war, many racketeers and black embezzlers sought to take advantage of the Ethiopian people. To remedy this situation a party of African-Americans, who belonged to the organisation called the Menelek Club, visited H.I.M Emperor Haile Selassie I at His residence in Bath, England, in 1936. They informed His Majesty of the large sums of money being raised in the United States by unauthorised persons in the name of Ethiopia.

Impressed by them, His Majesty decided to send one of His Special Envoys to the United States to co-ordinate the collection of all funds for Ethiopia. He selected His personal physician, Dr Malaku Bayen who was also a relative of the Emperor and had served His Majesty in his early years as a page and personal attendant. In 1922, Malaku Bayen had entered the USA to study medicine. Because of the crisis in Ethiopia, His Majesty recalled the physician in July 1935. However, for the second time, His Majesty saw the need to send Dr Bayen to the USA, this time as His Emissary to Black America.

From the time of his return to the United States in September 1936, Dr Bayen had been working in conjunction with the Black organisation, United Aid for Ethiopia, which was the most active of the few remaining Ethiopian aid associations. The situation began to change, however, as members of the American Communist Party took sharp interest in the United Aid and attempted to transform it into a communist front.

Wanting to be free of any entanglement with the Communists, whether black or white, Dr Bayen and others decided to form an entirely new organisation to be known as the Ethiopian World Federation. With Malaku Bayen as its executive head, the Ethiopian World Federation, Inc. (EWF Inc) was formally created on the 25 August 1937. Dr Lorenzo King was then elected the first president. By 1940 there were twenty-two branches in existence, some of which were located in the West Indies. Its membership was said to be in the thousands, and was largely drawn from many Black nationalist organisation; many were supporters of Garvey's movement, the UNIA, which was severely weakened, following his imprisonment and deportation from the USA.

The preamble of the Ethiopian World Federation, Inc., states: "We, the Black People of the World, in order to effect Unity, Solidarity, Liberty, Freedom and Self-determination, to secure Justice and maintain the Integrity of Ethiopia, which is our divine heritage, do hereby establish and ordain this Constitution for the Ethiopian World Federation, Incorporated."

Later, and influenced by the EWF, the church published the following affirmation:
We affirm that Ethiopia is the ancestral home of more than four hundred million black people of the world dating back to the Garden of Eden, which was the ancient land of Ethiopia, and later as the race increased they spread out over the entire continent of Africa.

We affirm that Ethiopia is the oldest Empire on earth today and that we black people are direct descendants of the Prophets Moses, King David, King Solomon and Queen of Sheba.

We affirm that His Imperial Majesty Emperor Haile Selassie I of Ethiopia is the only living King; a direct descendant of King David sitting on the throne of Ethiopia today. We affirm that the Ark of the Covenant, which was taken to Ethiopia by Menelik, son of King Solomon and the Queen of Sheba, is still under the protection of His Imperial Majesty Haile Selassie I, who is a great Prophet and the true representative of the Spirit of Jesus Christ on earth this day.

In 1955 Mrs Maymie Richardson, the International Organiser of the Ethiopian World Federation, Inc. went to Jamaica on behalf of the headquarters in the US to expound the doctrine and organise eleven new locals of the EWF, Inc. In the same year the International Executive of the EWF, Inc. wrote to the executives of all locals, informing them that His Majesty Emperor Haile Selassie I had granted 500 acres of fertile land, through the Ethiopian World Federation,Inc., to the Black people of the West who aided Ethiopia during her time of distress. Since then various members of the Rastafarian community have functioned in this organisation.

11. Ethiopian World Federation, Inc Local 33

The establishment of Local 33 of the Ethiopian World Federation, Inc. has been a major and historic development within the history of the Rastafarian community in England. And it was the efforts of the membership of Local 33 which brought the Ethiopian Orthodox Church, one of the oldest in Christendom, to the shores of Britain. With the emergence of the Ethiopian World Federation, Inc. in London, the membership began to increase rapidly. General meetings were held all over London and the Midlands, which had large Black communities, mostly at the request of youths who wanted to know more about the doctrine of Rastafari, and the history of the EWF, Inc.

The members of Local 33 were now actively working within an institution of Ethiopia for the first time and this helped to increase the prestige of the Movement in the early seventies. One of the first major function of Local 33 was fund raising on behalf of the Ethiopian Orthodox Church in Jamaica. Until then all functions which were held to celebrate any national Ethiopian holiday were just for the benefit of the members. But this changed with the establishment of the EWF, Inc.

The first public celebration held by the EWF, Inc. Local 33 was entitled *"A Grand Rastafarian Ball"* and was held on 22nd September 1972 at Woodland Hall, Acton, London W3. It was an impressive event, with the stage draped in the national colours of Ethiopia, Green, Gold and Red. The main attraction of the programme was the now legendary reggae singer U-Roy, and hundreds of people turned out for the event.

It was the first time the Rastafarian community in London had attempted anything on this scale and presentation. It seemed to coincide with the mood of the time and was to set a precedent for future celebrations of Ethiopian National holidays, of which the three main ones are 23rd July, The Emperor Haile Selassie I of Ethiopia's birthday; 2nd November, Coronation Day and 7th January, Ethiopian Christmas, which are observed by Rastafarians universally.

The building at 356 Portobello Rd W10 was now transformed into the HQ of the Rastafarian activities in England. To the brethren and sistren who were members of this organisation, the Charter and Constitution they had received from the Federation headquarters in New York was recognition and legitimacy, in their eyes, for their activities. As a rule the Charter was displayed at all meetings of Local 33 (EWF, Inc.) for the benefit of new members and also as proof of the organisation's legitimacy.

A weekly newsheet was also published by the Federation called "Emperor Yohannes Local 33 Weekly News". This helped to keep the membership informed on developments within the Movement in Jamaica and England and also outlined the role and general policy of the organ. For example, issue No. 3 carried a brief article on a meeting which was held in Birmingham in November 1972. The meeting was held at Digbeth Hall, Birmingham on Sunday 19th November 1972 by the EWF Inc. Local 33. Chairperson, Sister Wozero Bayrea* opened the meeting, which began with prayer and the singing of the Universal Ethiopian Anthem. Speakers were P Letang, General Secretary, R Prince, who spoke on Education and Culture, and A Foxe, President, who dealt with the role of the Federation (the text of his speech is reproduced in the following pages). The brothers and sisters at the meeting responded very well by asking a lot of questions and some

*Footnote: Sis Wozero Bayrea is now known as Sis. Wolette Mahdin.

applied for membership. At the end of the meeting they asked that a date should be set for a return meeting in the near future.

By the early part of 1973 a new generation of hard-core Rastafarian youth had emerged within the Federation. They made up almost the entire executive and membership and were representative of that generation of Black youth who had come to Britain in their early teens in the early and mid-sixties.

They had began to assert themselves against a racist society through the concept of Haile Selassie I as the true and living God, without any apologies. In so doing, they cemented the foundation for the future generation of Black youths in Britain who wish to maintain certain fundamental aspects of their cultural identity. The rapid grown of the Movement was already causing concern and hysteria amongst the parents and families of these youths, especially those from Jamaica, who held certain negative views on Rastafari. However, for the first time, the presence of Rastafarians was becoming more obvious to the Black communities in London's inner cities, and Birmingham in the Midlands.

With the development of the EWF, Inc., Local 33 however, the general policy had not changed much from the early sixties. This was due largely to the fact that Ascento Foxe, the President of the Local, and one of the original brethren from the late 50s, had always maintained that his directive from the Imperial Ethiopian Government, as a result of meetings at the London Embassy in the early 60s, is to return to Jamaica and help with the development of the Movement. And there was no policy for Brethren who wanted to migrate to Ethiopia / Africa.

The Role of the Federation by A. Foxe

Hail Brothers and Sisters, Greetings to you in the name of Eyesus Kristos, Haile Selassie I.

Today Brothers and Sisters we, the Black People of the West Indies, have for the first time in our lives an Organisation that will help us to uplift our social standard and give us that pride in ourselves as a people. Who for the past four hundred years have been ruled and reduced to the status of West Indians by our so-called masters the so-called civilised race.

For centuries we were taught to look to England for leadership, for education and for the whole development of ourselves. We were even taught that Africa was a jungle ruled by savages. This helped to distort the minds of our mothers and fathers, that they were ashamed that their fore-parents were Africans. The divide and rule principle gave us a cosmopolitan culture that let us become dependent on the plantation owners, in this time known as the managers for the Banana Industry.

Our brothers and sisters were forced to accept charity from most of the nations in the world because of the rape of our Motherland, Africa. We have seen in the early sixties the West Indies were given independence, yet the ruling class was chosen by the power who have the most investment in the country. Our sons and daughters were still being taught the history of Sir Francis Drake, Cecil Rhodes and Livingstone. The curriculum of the country was still drafted up by the colonial masters. To be educated in London was the cry of the day, the whole expectation of our life was decided in London.

Today the whole question of the advancement of our people in England and the West Indies comes under question. We have seen Europe organising into the EEC (European Economic Community) who is in no way committing their Government to any strong economical ties with Ethiopia-Africa. The whole survival of the youth of the day becomes a problem because of no direction from our leaders. Yet when we look in Angola and South West Africa we see the youth playing an active part in the development of the struggle, politically, by fighting the imperialist where it hurts. In South East Asia the youths are fighting and helping to build their country. Yet in the West Indies the youths have become dependent on the hand-outs of the establishment.

Today the Ethiopian World Federation, Inc. has come to erase these decadent behaviour, it comes to inculcate and to correct the situation and give the youths that pride in themselves, a people whose nation is the fountain-head of civilisation. A nation whose contribution to world peace and security stands out. Today the Ethiopian World Federation, Inc. is here with the help of the Ethiopian Orthodox Church to give us the Black People the direction to spiritual happiness and to liberate our minds from the foreign doctrine that for four hundred years has been the instrument of the colonial power.

Reproduced from

(EWF Inc.) Emperor Yohannes Weekly News No. 3.

12. Delegation to New York and Jamaica 1973

a. Delegation to New York 1973

In February 1973 Local 33 received communication from Abba L Mandefro, head administrator of the Ethiopian Orthodox Church (EOC) in the West, based in New York.

He said that the membership should be informed of the forthcoming visit of His Holiness Abuna Theophilos, Patriarch of the Ethiopian Orthodox Church, to the USA and Jamaica. He also emphasised the importance of London being represented on this historic occasion, as this was His Holiness' first visit to the West since he was elected Patriarch in April 1971.

Within the next few months, the membership of Local 33 did some vigorous fund raising, along with voluntary contribution from each member. It was decided that five members of the executive would make up the delegation to the U.S. for His Holiness' visit. The task at the time seemed quite exciting to some of the members, and the result of the first delegation helped to increase the confidence of Brethren and Sistren within the organisation.

On Friday 11th May 1973 the delegation of five members left London for America in time for the ecumenical visit of His Holiness. They were Ascento-Pinto-Foxe, President; Roy Prince, 2nd Vice-President, Keith-Shaggy-Berry, Information Officer; N W Adams (Jah Blue), Sergeant-at-Arms, and Sis. Veronica Foxe, Women's Auxiliary. On arrival, the delegation was taken to a large building at the corner of Montgomery Avenue, Upper Bronx, NY. It contained several apartments, and was the International Head Quarters of the Ethiopian World Federation, as well as the temporary site of the Ethiopian Orthodox Church (EOC). The building also housed several dignitaries of the church including Abba L Mandefro and Abuna

Athanasius, Archbishop of the EOC in the western hemisphere, who officially resides in Trinidad, but was present for the occasion.

We were met by Mr George E Bryan, the International President of the Ethiopian World Federation, Inc., and two deacons of the EOC. The delegation had an informal discussion with Mr Bryan after everyone had been introduced.

On Saturday 12th May 1973 the delegation met the following dignitaries: His Grace Abuna Athanasius, Archbishop of the Ethiopian Orthodox Church in the West; Abba Yohannes, and Abba Petros. After the introduction by Abba L Mandefro, His Grace was given a report on the activities of the Brethren in London and their desire to have the Ethiopian Orthodox Church established there. During the discussion that followed, His Grace said he would be willing to accompany Abba Mandefro to London to establish the Church and ordain Rastafarian brethren as deacons.

The following day, Sunday 13th May 1973, the delegation attended a church service which lasted for four hours. Many new faithful were baptised into the church, including Keith-Shaggy-Berry, Sis. V Foxe and Roy Prince. After the service Abba Mandefro thanked the delegations from London and Canada for attending this historic occasion. He went on to announce the date of His Holiness' visit and announced also, that His Majesty Emperor Haile Selassie I would be visiting the country shortly, as the official guest of President Nixon.

Arrival of His Holiness Abuna Theophilos

On Monday 14th May the delegation gave Mr Bryan a report and other documents dealing with the Ethiopian

World Federation, Inc. Local 33 in London. Final plans were then made for the reception, the following day, of the PATRIARCH.

On Tuesday 15th May 1973 His Holiness Abuna Theophilos, Patriarch of the Ethiopian Orthodox Church, arrived at Kennedy Airport, New York, to a tremendous welcome from members of the EOC and the Rastafarian Community. He was greeted by two officials of the American Government and several church dignitaries from the Greek, Syrian and Armenian Orthodox Churches. After the official protocol had been exchanged, followed by a brief speech from His Holiness, the reception came to an end. The next few days the delegation attended various functions held on behalf of His Holiness.

On Sunday 20th May a major service was held at the St John Divine Cathedral, 11 St Amsterdam Ave, NY City, one of the biggest church buildings in America. The sermon was taken from Acts of the Apostles (Chapter 8:26-39, *Phillip and the Ethiopian "Eunuch"*) and was read by His Holiness. He said that the performance of the service which we had participated in was interpreted as the drama of salvation. The congregation was large and was represented by members of the other Orthodox Communities. After the service His Holiness laid a shrine of the Ethiopian Orthodox Church in the Cathedral. It was a glorious and colourful event.

On Tuesday 22nd May the delegation attended a meeting of the Ethiopian World Federation, Inc. Lion of Judah Local 1, chaired by Mr George E Bryan the International President. Mr Bryan gave a brief history of the Federation and dealt with the aims and objectives. He emphasised that more youth should embrace the Federation, and work though the constitution to achieve their objectives. Mr Bryan also said he was impressed with the works of the brethren in London, from what he had heard from Abba Mandefro, and the written reports he had received.

There was a lively debate afterwards. The brethren from New York were represented by Bro Habte Selassie, Rasta activist and deacon of the EOC, who led the discussion, and highlighted some of the problems that affected the Rastafari Community in America. After the meeting most of the assembly applied for membership of the Ethiopian World Federation, Inc. The delegation was also given certain documents of authorisation to help in the preparation for His Holiness' visit to Jamaica.

b. Delegation to Jamaica 1973

On Thursday 24th May 1973 the delegation from London (EWF Inc. Local 33) left New York for Jamaica. On arrival, the delegation was met by Bro. Wally, a Rastafari elder, who took us to the Ethiopian Orthodox Church rectory. Letters giving the delegation authority to help in the preparation for the Patriarch's visit to Jamaica was given to the priest in charge, Abba Watson.

Over the next few days the delegation attended various meetings with members of the Rastafari community, including the Rastafarian Movement Association (RMA) and the House of Theocracy at Bull Bay, Eastern Kingston.

On Wednesday 30th May 1973 the delegation attended a meeting at Success Hall, 63 Wildman Street in Kingston. Over 500 people were present; most were members of the Ethiopian Orthodox Church and the EWF Inc. The meeting was chaired by Cecil G Gordon, the Second International President of the EWF Inc., and speakers included Bro. J N Hibbert, one of the original architects of the Rastafari Movement, and three members of the London delegation, Bro. A Foxe, Keith Berry and N W Adams (Jah Blue).

The meeting was an attempt to revitalise the Ethiopian World Federation, Inc. as a social and political organisation, to embrace the social development of the Rastafarian community and members of the Ethiopian Orthodox Church. The audience was also told of the rapid growth of the Rastafari community in England, and the need for closer co-operation. A Foxe read out a resolution from Local 33 to the audience and this was well received (see resolution at the end of the next chapter).

On Sunday 3rd June the delegation attended a meeting at the Ethiopian Orthodox Church rectory. Present were members of the Board of Trustee, and a few deacons of the church. The meeting was presided over by Abba M Mandifro, who praised the delegation for their contribution and effort during His Holiness' visit in America. He also outlined the programme for His Holiness' reception ,and the duties of each officer, while His Holiness was in Jamaica.

Abuna Theophilos in Jamaica

On Wednesday 6th June, 1973 hundreds of people were present at Maxfield Park, Western Kingston, the permanent site for the Ethiopian Orthodox Church in Kingston, Jamaica, for the service by His Holiness Abuna Theophilos. The Jamaican Council of Churches was represented, along with two officials of the Government. After the sermon His Holiness emphasised the need for the Ethiopian community abroad to educate themselves. He then laid the corner stone for the EOC church building.

Many leading Brethren from the Rastafarian community were present, and the day ended with drumming and chanting from the large gathering which had attended this historic occasion. Mortimer Planno and members of the Nyahbinghi House led the drumming and chanting.

13. Charter 15 - Twelve Tribes of Israel

On Saturday 19th June 1973, the delegation attended a meeting at Ninth Street, Trench Town, with members and executives of an organisation, known then as Charter 15. The meeting was part of the directive, given to the London delegation, to inform the various groups to play a more active part within the Ethiopian World Federation, Inc. and the Ethiopian Orthodox Church. The members of Charter 15 were informed that the delegation was authorised by Abba L Mandefro, and was empowered to make recommendations on their behalf. The two main areas of contention with this group were:

(1) Their charter which gave them the right to function as the EWF Inc. was illegal.

(2) A dispute had developed between them and Abba Mandefro over the question of their baptism within the Orthodox Church.

One of the executive, Bro. Simeon, said that they had eventually found out that their charter was invalid and they were in the process of correcting the situation when a misunderstanding between themselves and Abba Mandefro developed.

At the time Charter 15 was strongly pro-orthodox. After the discussion, they said they embraced all that the delegation had said, but could make no decision until their President, Bro. Doctor (later known as Prophet Gad), had returned from Ethiopia.

After the meeting with the Brethren of Charter 15 the delegation from London spent the remaining days in the island attending various gatherings and meeting the personalities within the Movement.

On Wednesday 13th June 1973 the delegation left Jamaica for a week's stay in America before returning to London. During our visit at the International Headquarters of the Federation (EWF Inc.) a series of informal discussions took place between Mr George E Bryan, the International President, and members of the Rasta Community in New York, and the delegation.

On Saturday 16th June 1973 an Executive Meeting of the Ethiopian World Federation, Inc., Lion of Judah Local 1 took place at the International HQ. Mr Bryan chaired the meeting and went on to appoint four members of the delegation as International Officers of the Ethiopian World Federation, Inc. The four were Ascento Foxe as the 1st International President; Keith-Shaggy-Berry as Int. Information Officer; Roy Prince as Int. Chaplain and Gabre Wold-Adams as Int. Director of Youth Units. These appointments were endorsed by the executive of the EWF and Abba L Mandefro, Head Administrator of Ethiopian Orthodox Church in the West. Two days later, the delegation returned to London.

Delegation Returned to England

The return of four international officers of the Ethiopian World Federation, Inc. Local 33 was a significant achievement in the development of the Rastafarian Community in London. New contacts were made with members of the Rastafarian Community in the US and Canada.

Abba Mandefro had been to Canada the previous year, in July 1972, to officially establish a branch of the Ethiopian Orthodox Church in Toronto. The delegation was told by Abba Mandefro how, during the middle of this event, the Toronto police insisted that he stop and clear the church, because they had received a call saying a bomb was in the building. After the search the police said it must be the work of a prankster, as no bomb was found on the premises. It was a typical example of the kind of harassment the Rastafarian Communities were experiencing in those early times.

The visit of the Patriarch of the Ethiopian Orthodox Church to Jamaica was second only to the Emperor's in April 1966. However it was one of the first events which attracted Rastafarians living outside Jamaica, and served to develop more consciousness within the Movement in its international perspective. There were also closer relationships between groups such as The Rastafarian Movement Association (RMA) and Local 33 in London.

The members of Local 33 were given a full report on the activities of the delegation.The news that the Ethiopian Orthodox Church would be officially established the following year in London, by Abba Mandefro and His Grace Abuna Athanasius, Bishop of the EOC in the West, was well received.

In July 1973 shortly after the delegation had returned to London, Bro. A Foxe and Gabre-Wold Adams had an informal discussion with Vernon Carrington (Bro. Doctor) President of Charter 15, who had stopped off briefly in London on his return to Jamaica from Ethiopia. Also present was Pepe Judah who had accompanied Bro. Doctor over to west London. Bro. Doctor said the purpose of his visit to Ethiopia was to examine conditions on the Land in Shashamane and the possibilities of members of charter 15 migrating to live there. He was informed by A. Foxe about the recent developments during His Holiness' visit and was told to deal with the validity of his charter.

Bro. Doctor returned to Jamaica and resumed negotiations with Abba Mandefro, concerning their charter, and relationship with the Ethiopian Orthodox Church (EOC).

However these negotiations did not work out and in the later part of 1974 Charter 15 was dissolved and became known as the Twelve Tribes of Israel Organisation. Bro. Doctor as the founder is called Prophet Gad.

In London Pepe Judah, who had began to identify with Charter 15 during the later part of 1973, was now meeting regularly with a group of Brethren in the south-east London area; these included Ras Binghi and some members of the Ethiopian World Federation. This was at 28 St Agnes Place, SE11. When Twelve Tribes emerged in Jamaica, Pepe became quite influential with its development in England.

By the end of 1973 the executive of Local 33 had established contact with the Kensington Council of Churches . The purpose of this was to inform them of their intention to establish a branch of the Ethiopian Orthodox Church in London, and their desire for a church building on a temporary basis until they could secure one of their own. The negotiations with Rev. Dennin, the pastor of the Methodist Church at Kingsdown Close W11, was eventually successful and the membership of (EWF, Inc.) Local 33 was allowed to use the Methodist Church premises, Kingsdown Close for their Church Services on a Sunday afternoon.

These developments opened new areas of contact with various members of the Church of England establishment, many of whom welcomed the development of the Ethiopian Orthodox Church in Britain.

The congregation at the Sunday Service was growing as each month went by. There was also support from some of the older members of the Black community who were now attending quite regularly. They represented a minority within Afro-Caribbean community who always adhered to the concept of an indigenous African Church. Although they did not share the belief of the Rastafarians in the Divinity of Haile Selassie I, nevertheless their presence added to the whole development of the Church. This was a common feature of the Ethiopian Church in the West.

An Anglican priest who had heard of the presence of the Ethiopian Orthodox Church, and came to observe the members in worship, said he was quite impressed with the participation of so many young people in the EOC Service, and found the experience rewarding. He also remarked that it was the opposite in his Church.

Ethiopian World Federation, Incorporated,
356 Portobello Road(1974).

Coronation of His Imperial Majesty Emperor Haile Selassie I and Empress Menen 2nd November 1930

Marcus Mosiah Garvey

The Rastafari Community in London receive the Charter of the Ethiopian World Federation, Inc. (1972).

Left to Right: Norman W Adams (Jah Blue) and Ras Ascento Foxe (Bro Pinto).

Abba L. M. Mandefro

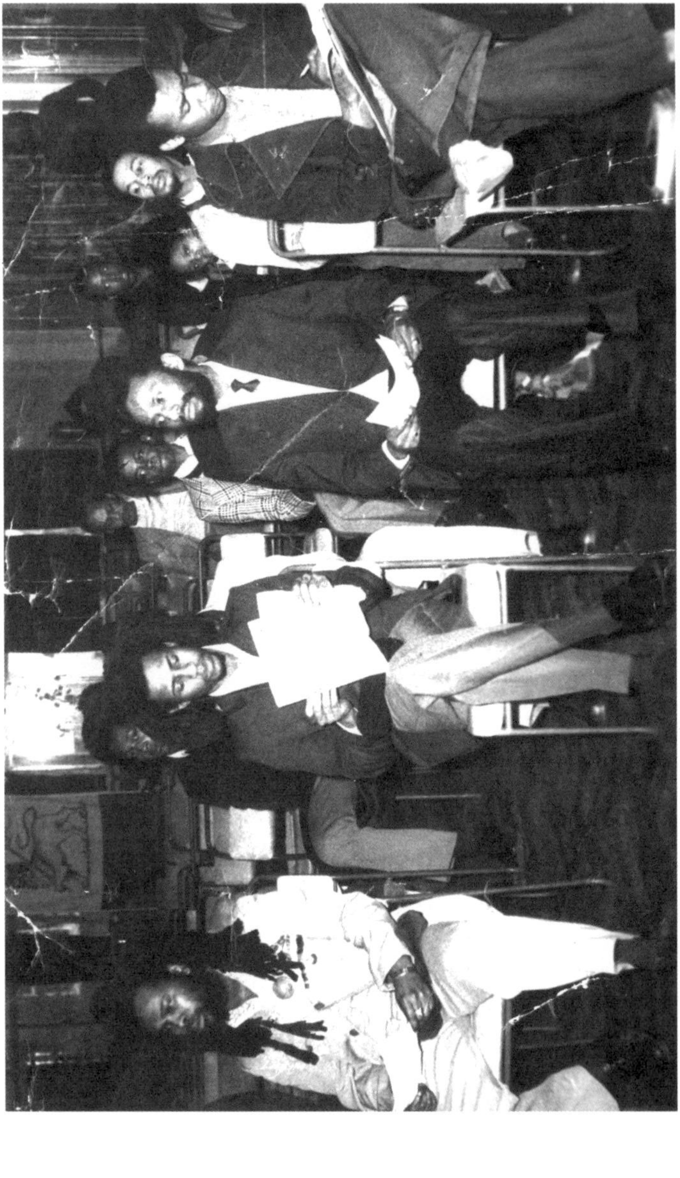

The First Rasta Conference in London was held at the Loyola Hall in Tottenham, north London (1974).

ETHIOPIAN BISHOP VISITS LONDON

Monday, 19th August, 1974. His Grace Abuna Samuel, Bishop of the Ethiopian Orthodox Church, arrived at Heathrow Airport, London en route to Ethiopia from the World Federation of Churches in Brussels.

He was invited here by the Ethiopian World Federation Inc. Emperor Yohannes Local 33 in London, and was welcomed enthusiastically at Heathrow Airport by members of the Federation and the Trustee Board for the Ethiopian Orthodox Church in London, and was driven to the home of the Chairman of the Ethiopian World Federation in London, Otto Emmanual Fox, where he stayed throughout his visit.

His visit was planned to last one week but owing to pressing matters at home, he had to cut short his visit. Abuna Samuel is the "Second Highest" in the Ethiopian Orthodox Church and his historical visit to the newly established Orthodox Church in this Country is a remarkable memorial to the faithful of the Orthodox faith in this country and, indeed, throughout the world.

TROUBLES

He expressed his regrets that he was unable to fulfil the period which was planned but, owing to the seriousness of the trouble at present in Ethiopia, he felt that his duty lay back home and therefore had to return as soon as possible.

Abba Samuel expressed his delight at the way in which the members of the church were actively participating in establishing the Orthodox Church and its principles and beliefs in this Country, for it was only a short while ago, to be precise, May 24, 1974, that Abba Mandefrow, the Ethiopian Orthodox Church Bishop of the West from America, arrived in London to establish the Church. His Grace made it clear that it was the intention of His Holiness, the Archbishop, to support morally and physically the Ethiopian Orthodox Church now being established in the West.

For some time, Abba Samuel has been living in the West Indies, America and Russia. His first public meeting was held at the Ethiopian World Federation Building at 356 Portobello Road, London W.10, on Tuesday, August 21st. At this meeting he was questioned by a large congregation of baptized members of the Church and proceeded to give lectures and teachings on this ancient Church now being established in this Country.

DIFFERENCES

He was an overwhelming success and owing to the fact that he had to leave hurriedly on Thursday morning, we made sure that he had had sufficient rest and were able to meet him again for service at our Church at Lancaster Road, W.10, on Wednesday August 22, for his farewell service. Many faithful followers of the Church from the Midlands and all over London were present and the church was packed to almost capacity.

The service was conducted by Abbona Samuel, for the most part in Gees and we had been instructed the previous night on the differences between the English translation and Gees. Finally, at the end of the service, a vast congregation of approximately 200 to 300 were given the opportunity to meet His Grace and to bid him farewell. We all expressed our great thanks to almighty God for granting us this opportunity and hoped that we would one day be honoured by the visit of His Holiness, the head of the Ethiopian Orthodox Church. His Grace assured us that on his return to Ethiopia, he would fulfil perhaps the greatest of our needs which was to have a permanent priest of our own residing in this Country as head of our church and he felt sure that this would be possible in the very near future.

PROGRESS

I would conclude that the historical event which took place on August 19, 1974, will mark a tremendous step forward in the self determination of a minority people within this community in expressing a desire to fulfil their hereditary rights. The Ethiopian Orthodox Church and the Ethiopian World Federation are not merely superficial outlets, but are, in reality, embedded within the souls of the young generation of Afro descent in this Country and guides them along the path of fulfilment; a path which can only be made manifest through the works and endeavours of us all at this present time.

Left to Right Standing: L Thompson, P Letang, R Prince, A Foxe, N W Adams,
Bottom Row: A Wilkinson, E Luke and T Lewis after E O C service, Lancaster Road, west London.

The People's Democratic Movement (political wing of the Rastafari Movement) 1971.

'Dreadlock' court verdict makes legal history

USA, NEW YORK
New York State's highest court says the wearing of dreadlocks by Rastafarians is protected under the United States constitution.

As a result of the ruling, a Westindian who hasn't cut his hair in 20 years because of his Rastafarian beliefs, cannot be forced by prison officials to cut his dreadlocks.

The unanimous 7-0 ruling in the case of 32 year old Alfredo Lewis was made by the Court of Appeals of the State of New York.

The court said Lewis who is serving a five-to-ten year sentence for the killing of his sister-in-law, was sincere in his religious beliefs and therefore his hair was protected by the first amendment guarantees of freedom of expression and religion.

Lewis had refused to allow prison officials to cut his hair.

The New York State Department of Corrections wanted to cut his hair in keeping with a policy that required prison inmates to get crewcuts and shaves for pictures as part of prison entry security procedures.

The haircut and shave policy which has since been changed, allowed inmates to grow their hair as long as they desired after the initial entry pictures had been taken.

The Westindian who was serving his sentence at the Clinton State Prison was able to convince the seven judge panel that he believed his strength was derived from his hair and it was therefore protected by the US Constitution.

In its opinion, the court said that Lewis was "sincere in his beliefs that are of a religious nature and that a haircut would impinge on those beliefs."

On top of that, the court argued that the corrections department had failed to prove that a haircut and a shave were important security factors to merit ignoring the Westindian's First Amendment rights.

Lewis who lived in Queens, New York City, before going to prison last May, was convicted of manslaughter after his sister-in-law died in a shooting incident in July, 1984.

.O. Ref. C.S.P. 99

AMAICA

DESPATCH NO. 637

10th June, 1959

Sir,

I have the honour to refer to demi-official correspondence between Sir Hugh Foot and Mr. H. Phillips of the Colonial Office, ending with the latter's confidential letter WIS 1025/6/01 of the 9th November, 1956, and to address you on the subject of the Ras Tafari movement in Jamaica.

2. This movement is not to be confused with the agitation being sponsored by the Reverend C.V. Henry, about whom I have addressed you in my secret despatch No. 636 of today's date. The Ras Tafari movement and the Reverend C.V. Henry have a common platform to the extent that they both advocate a return to Africa for their followers in Jamaica; but whereas Mr. Henry is a charlatan who is preying on the simple people of Jamaica, the Ras Tafari movement has a definite historical background.

3. The Ras Tafari movement is understood to date from the time of the war between Italy and Abyssinia - a war which provoked in the West Indies strong feelings against European colonial powers. As a result of this feeling and of the depressed conditions in the West Indies at that time, a group of persons established what might be called almost a "religious sect" which (in their ignorance of geography) recognised the Emperor Haile Selassie as King of Africa and also ascribed to him divine characteristics. It is probable that the movement also had, and indeed still has, some religious significance; as it is understandable that coloured people living in depressed conditions and encouraged by agitators to develop antagonism against the white race, should wish to see their god in the person of a coloured man.

4. During the years since the establishment of this movement, it has developed into a number of comparatively small groups of men living in different parts of the country, though mainly in Kingston, who worship Haile Selassie and talk repeatedly about their ultimate return to their "homeland" in Africa. The followers of the movement do not shave (presumably in order to copy the beard of the Emperor Haile Selassie); they quote, or rather misquote, the Bible in order to prove that their belief in their destiny is correct; they live in the most squalid surroundings and it has hitherto been impossible to persuade any of them to move into new housing areas; and they hold frequent meetings at which they quote the scriptures in extravagant terms, sing racial hymns and smoke ganja. Though some of the followers of the movement are sincere, if somewhat mentally unbalanced, it is hardly surprising that they should collect around themselves some of the riffraff of the country - people who find that by living in squalor and by cultivating or trading in ganja they are able to make a livelihood without doing any work. It is also hardly surprising that a movement of this nature comes into conflict with the forces of law and order, and that its followers are traditionally hostile to the Police and indeed hostile to the established government of Jamaica. They are indeed a potential source of danger, as was shown by the recent riot in the Coronation market in Kingston, reported in the Monthly Intelligence Report for May.

ppendix I

5. A close watch is always maintained on the activities of the movement, and I enclose a copy of the latest appreciation dated the 13th January, 1959, prepared jointly by the Security Liaison Officer and the Special Branch and approved by the Local Standing Intelligence Committee.

6. In the long term there is little doubt that the only method of suppressing the movement will be by sociological means, and indeed various attempts have been made by religious and other leaders of the community in the

past/

The Right Honourable
Alan Lennox-Boyd, M.P.,
Secretary of State for the Colonies

S E C R E T

26

past to direct the beliefs of these unfortunate people into more reasonable channels. These efforts have hitherto borne no fruit; but it is interesting to record that a group of Ras Tafarians has recently been invited to visit the current Moral Rearmament conference at Mackinaw in Canada, in the hope that some impression may be made upon them not only by the leaders of M.R.A., but also by Africans who are understood to be attending the same conference. It is not yet known whether the local representatives of the Moral Rearmament Movement will arrange this visit.

7. In due course, and when the General Election in Jamaica is over, further consideration will be given to the possibility of setting up a committee to examine the social and economic background to this problem. It is already clear, however, that no real impact will be made on the minds of these people unless they can be convinced that their faith in a return to Africa is misconceived and that their belief that they will be welcomed on their return by the Emperor Haile Selassie is without foundation.

ppendix II
ppendix III

8. In this connection I enclose a copy of a letter dated the 30th of May, 1959, addressed to the Editor of the "Daily Gleaner", protesting about the terms of a leading article, of which a copy is also enclosed. This letter emanates from a Jamaican branch of the Ethiopian World Federation Inc. which is stated to have been founded in the United States. In fact the letter is from one of the numerous groups of the Ras Tafari movement in Jamaica. The editor of the "Daily Gleaner" has himself addressed the Government of Ethiopia in the matter and I enclose a copy of his letter.

ppendix IV

9. The purpose of this despatch is to enquire whether Her Majesty's Government would be able to approach the Government of Ethiopia in order to secure a definite statement that that Government and the Emperor of Ethiopia have no interest whatsoever in these unfortunate and misguided people in Jamaica; and that there can be no question of them being admitted to Ethiopia either now or in the future. I can well appreciate that it may not be possible to make such an approach, but both the Chief Minister and I will be most grateful if the matter can be examined. I would only add that Sir Hugh Foot made a demi-official approach on similar lines to the British Ambassador in Ethiopia on the 16th August, 1956. I attach a copy of his letter. I have been unable to trace that any reply was ever received.

ppendix V

10. I am sending a copy of this despatch to the Governor-General.

I have the honour to be,
Sir,
Your most obedient, humble Servant,

K.W. Blackburne

GOVERNOR

Resolution from Ethiopian World Federation Inc.

Emperor Yohannes Local 33

Whereas the Church cannot take part in the politics of Jamaica, reason being non-political, We the Officers and Members of the Ethiopian World Federation Inc. Emperor Yohannes Local 33, hereby present this resolution for the creation of a strong and collective Branch of the Ethiopian World Federation Inc. to be established in Jamaica. To help and co-operate with the Ethiopian Orthodox Church, in the social development of its members and the people as a whole.

The first branch of the Federation to be established in Jamaica was Local 17 in 1938, also other different branches with Local 31 being established in 1942, but the implementation of the Ethiopian World Federation Inc. policies were not fully utilised. Reasons being:-

1 The expounders of the Federation's policy in Jamaica. Their minds were not fully developed to the importance of Organisation activities relevant to the Social and Economical needs of the Community at that time.

2 Too many different Locals of the Federation in Jamaica, which created local groupism with different ideological interpretation of their own, which was not compatible with the constitution and objectives of the Federation.

3 The Rastafarians, before 1955, could not identify themselves positively with the Federation. This was caused by the unorthodox prevention of equal participation in the activities of the already established locals of the Ethiopian World Federation, Inc.

4 The past history of the established Local's behaviour towards Rastafarians, causing suspicion from the overwhelming force of the Rastafarian Movement, who are fully aware of the role the Federation plays in the social and spiritual development of the people who acclaim Ethiopia as their ancestral home, compatible with article 1 sections 2a and 3 and the preamble of the Ethiopian World Federation Inc. Constitution and By-laws.

Findings: *We the Officers and members of the Ethiopian World Federation Inc., Emperor Yohannes Local 33, London Branch believe, after careful study, the time has come when we should bring to the attention of the dignitaries of the Ethiopian Orthodox Church and International Officers of the Ethiopian World Federation Inc., the importance of the creation of an effective branch of the Ethiopian World Federation Inc., working with the Ethiopian Orthodox Church in Jamaica, in the fulfilment of the Church and Federation aims and objectives.*

Today the Rastafarians must be given the right of involvement within the policy making of the Federation, owing to the fact, as statistics will show, that the majority of members baptised into the Church in Jamaica are, in fact, Rastafarians.

Today the Federation must re-organise itself to meet the present situation in Jamaica and the International World. Whereas the Church is established in Jamaica, a young independent country, a country where the social, economical and political development is not fully advanced to meet the pressing needs of the people, which are as follows:

(1) Social welfare of the Community.

(2) The serious under-staffing of the already inadequate hospitals and medical facilities.

(3) The desperate needs for better housing.

(4) The indifference to the suffering and misfortune of a large number of the people.

(5) The extremely limited educational facilities and opportunities which are lacking within the area of the under-

privileged grassroot people, who constitute members of the Church, Federation and Rastafarians.

Today the Church presents a new era in the general development of the people of Jamaica. The Federation must take unto itself the responsibility to fulfil Article 1 Section 2 (a), (b), (c), (d), (e) and (h). In 1960, present members of the Ethiopian World Federation Inc. Emperor Yohannes Local 33 in England, became involved in the formation of a Sub-Local of Local 37. One of the Sub-Local's fundamental objectives was to involve the Federation in finding a working solution to fit the needs for the social and economical development of the Rastafarians in Jamaica.

Members of the Sub-Local visited the Ethiopian Embassy and the Cultural Attache who sympathised with their views. They then met the Ambassador, who undertook to become the mediator between Ethiopia and Rastafarian members of the Sub-Local. The name of one of the dignitaries of the Ethiopian Orthodox Church was given to them: Abba Habte Mariam Workeneh.

In the year 1963, present members of this delegation met Abba Habte Mariam Workeneh at the Imperial Ethiopian Embassy in London, where they discussed with Abba, the question of the establishment of an Ethiopian Orthodox Church in Jamaica, Rastafarian support to the Church and the question of the institutionalisation of the Rastafarian Movement under the banner of the Ethiopian World Federation Inc.

We were told by Abba that, on his return to Ethiopia, he would look into the question of the establishing of the Ethiopian Orthodox Church in Jamaica. He would also help to bring about the rights needed to enable the Rastafarians to participate actively in spiritual, social and economical community development.

Today we have seen the fulfilment of the Ethiopian Orthodox Church established in Jamaica, yet we have not seen an effectively strong branch of the Ethiopian World Federation Inc.

established in Jamaica, fulfilling the functions necessary for the growth and progress of the Ethiopian World Federation Inc. members and people generally.

Your Holiness the Patriarch Abba Theophilos, dignitaries of the Ethiopian Orthodox Church, Mr President and members of the Ethiopian World Federation Inc., we, the delegates and members of Emperor Yohannes Local 33, are now prepared to return to Jamaica and work with the Church to establish an effective branch of the Ethiopian World Federation Inc. in Jamaica, working with Local 1 in New York to participate in community development and social reforms.

We believe, that members of the Ethiopian World Federation Inc. should be involved in Local Government activities, so as to bring about the Federation's objectives, Article 1 Section 2 (a) to (h).

We believe that the active Rastafarian members of the Ethiopian World Federation Inc. should be given International Office within the Federation, so as to erase the suspicion from among Rastafarians and create that dialogue that is so needed and requisite in the solution of the needs of the Rastafarians, members of the Church and people of Jamaica.

We pray that this resolution will be accepted from our Local, Emperor Yohannes Local 33, in the light of our already active participations. We invoke the blessings of the Church in this great task ahead of us."

(Presented 30th May 1973 at meeting at Success Hall, 63 Wildman Street, Kingston Jamaica.)

14. The Ethiopian Orthodox Church

Before the introduction of Christianity into Ethiopia, Judaism was practised, as is related in the Kebra Negest (The Glory of Kings). It tells the story of how the Queen of Sheba visited King Solomon in Jerusalem and, on her return to Ethiopia, bore him a son, whom she named Menilek. When Menilek grew up he visited his father in Jerusalem and returned home accompanied by many Israelites, the sons of the Levites, as well as the Ark of the Covenant.

From then on, Judaism was practised in Ethiopia as the official state religion until it was eclipsed by Christianity. It is said by some authorities that the Falasha tribe of Northern Ethiopia, who practise a form of Judaism to this day, are descendants of the Israelites.

Christianity became the official religion of Ethiopia in the fourth century, but the religion was known in Ethiopia much earlier. In Acts of the Apostles 8: 27-39 we are told of a certain Eunuch, the Treasurer of Queen Candace of Ethiopia, who went to Jerusalem to worship the God of Israel. There he met Philip and was baptised by him. Ethiopian tradition asserts that he returned home and evangelised the gospel to the people.

Irenaeus writes that he preached the gospel to the Ethiopians. This was done to fulfil the prophecy of Psalms 68:31 *"Ethiopia shall stretch forth her hands unto God."*
The Ethiopian Orthodox Church (EOC) is one of the group of churches that believe in one nature of Jesus Christ. Since the Ecumenical Council of Chalcedon in 451 AD, the Church has retained its Christian faith, its ancient traditions, customs and way of life. It is in full communion with the Egyptian Orthodox Church, the Jacobite Church of Syria, the Syrian Orthodox Church of Malabar in India

and the Armenian Orthodox Church. The Church holds its own synod and elects its own Patriarchs, Bishops and Archbishops. The first Patriarch was His Holiness, Abuna Theophilos (until the Ethiopian Revolution in 1974).

The Church is a member of the World Council of Churches and has branches in other parts of the world such as Jerusalem, Sudan, New York and the West-Indies. For some members of the Rastafarian community the Ethiopian Orthodox Church has always been seen as an Ethiopian institution of which the Emperor is the Head, and an alternative to westernised churches. It came to Jamaica as a direct request of the Rastafarian community and members of the Ethiopian World Federation, Inc.

Establishment of the Ethiopian Orthodox Church (St. Mary of Zion) in Britain

The establishment of the Ethiopian Orthodox Church (EOC) in Britain has been a major accomplishment of the Rastafarian Community in west London during the early seventies. It was the accumulated efforts of Brethren and Sistren who wanted to worship in a traditional indigenous African Church. For many Brethren and Sistren it was a natural progression in identifying themselves with one of Ethiopia's ancient institutions, and according to Ethiopian tradition, His Majesty Haile Selassie I is Defender of the Faith. Another practical reason for wanting the EOC in London, was that Rastafari Brethren and their families always face discrimination from the establishment (Babylon) in terms of their faith.

For example, Rastafarian children were excluded from certain Church of England schools, or if they were unfortunate to go to prison, Rastafari was not accepted as a valid religion, therefore their religious freedom was withdrawn. Many even suffered their worst humiliation in having their dreadlocks cut.

On Friday 24th May, 1974 Abba Laike Mariam Mandefro* arrived at Heathrow Airport, London. He was met at the airport by members of the (EWF Inc.) Local 33, and driven to the home of A Foxe, where he stayed throughout his visit to London.

In the evening, Abba held his first general meeting at the HQ on Portobello Rd W10 where he met the members of Local 33 and the Rastafarian Community in general. Abba Mandefro opened the meeting with a prayer in which he gave God thanks for all his works. After this he talked about his first meeting with Foxe and Adams in Jamaica in 1972. He said he was introduced to the Brethren by the late Rev. Ascot, assistant priest in charge of the EOC in Jamaica, and was impressed by their attitude towards EWF, Inc. and the EOC. He also mentioned that His Grace Abuna Athanasius desired to come to London for the establishment of the EOC but had to cancel his trip, as he was called to Ethiopia.

After Abba Mandefro had finished his speech on his activities and the development of the EOC in the West, he was asked questions about the Land Shashamane in Ethiopia and also about Charter 15. Pepe Judah, Ras Malachi and Ras Binghi from St Agnes Place, were present.

On Sunday 26th May 1974 Abba Mandefro held the historic service that was to establish the Ethiopian Orthodox Church in England, called St Mary of Zion. The ceremony took place at Notting Hill Methodist Church, Lancaster Rd. W11. Dressed in traditional habit, Abba led the procession from outside the Church building into the Church, chanting *"The Lion of Judah shall break every chain."*

*Footnote: Abba L.M. Mandefro is now called Abuna Yesehaq, Archbishop of the western hemisphere EOC and resides in U.S.A.

The first sacrament to be performed was that of Baptism. Abba baptised many Rastafari Brethren and their families. After the Baptism Abba went on to administer the sacrament of Communion to all the faithful who were baptised. The Abba also performed the sacrament of Confirmation and explained the use of holy oil which he used to anoint all baptised into the Ethiopian Orthodox Church. He stated that the holy oil was prayed over for seven years before it could be used and dates back to King David and King Solomon of Israel.

During the service Abba was assisted by deacons R. Prince, A. Wilkinson, L. Thompson (Amde Zion), [1]T. Lewis and E. Luke. The service started at 1:30p.m. and lasted approximately 5 hours. After the service the members ate and drank as one big family. In America and England, this seems to be a feature of the Ethiopian Church. Food was prepared, as many members had to travel long distances to attend the Church.

Abba Mandefro also held a second service on Sunday 2nd June 1974 where more Brethren and Sistren were baptised. After the service Abba introduced Abba Tekle Mikael Abay, who was an Ethiopian priest studying in this country. He agreed to assist the members of the Church until a priest was sent from Ethiopia. A few days later Abba Mandefro returned to America, leaving the St. Mary of Zion EOC firmly established.

Three months later, the Ethiopian Orthodox Church in London was consolidated with a visit from His Grace Abuna Samuel. Abuna Samuel's position in the Ethiopian Orthodox Church hierarchy was second to His Holiness,

*Footnote:: (1) T Lewis is now Known as Tesfa Zion and is now the priest in charge of the EOC Clapham London.

the Patriarch of the Church of Ethiopia. The event was published in the EWF Inc. Local 33 monthly magazine (see clipping on earlier page).

Many of the Brethren and Sistren remember the Abuna and the impact he made during the farewell service held on his behalf at Lancaster Rd. W10, on 22nd August 1974. After the sermon he told the members of the church that one of his recommendations at the World Council of Churches in Brussels was for the freedom fighters in Southern Africa to be given arms to defend themselves and not only medicine. His Grace expressed his regrets for having cut short his visit but owing to the troubles in Ethiopia he had to return urgently. However, he assured the members that he would help us secure a priest from Ethiopia as soon as possible.

On his return to Ethiopia the members of the EOC in London heard several months later that he was killed during the civil unrest that had began to engulf Ethiopia. Many of us remember him with great affection and respect.

In October 1975 Abba Aregawi Wolde-Gabriel was sent from Ethiopia as the official priest in charge of St. Mary of Zion EOC in London. His presence amongst the members was a social and spiritual upliftment. The activities within the programme now included Bible classes, which examined the theology and concept of the Ethiopian Orthodox Church. Amharic, the national language of Ethiopia, was also taught one evening per week.

There was a new sense of pride and optimism amongst members of the Rastafarian Community involved with these developments. New contacts and information were sent to various institutional bodies informing them of the presence of the official priest in charge of the EOC in London.

It was during this period that arrangements were made to find an alternative base for Sunday service, as the Methodist Church had now become unsuitable. One of the reasons for this was that the EOC Sunday Service was conducted after 12 o'clock midday, after it was used in the morning by the regular users. Abba Wolde-Gabriel pointed out that our service should start before midday as this was in keeping with the tradition of the Church in Ethiopia.

Shortly after negotiations with various bodies and the North Kensington Council of Churches, the EOC moved and was given the use of the Ecumenical Centre, Denbigh Rd. W11, Westbourne Grove. This building was much more suited to the activities of the Church as it was more spacious and its service could start at the appropriate time. It was a period of growth and stability within the Church.

One of Abba Wolde-Gabriel's first and important negotiations was a meeting held on Tuesday 22nd March 1976 at the Home Office with the Chaplain General of HM Prisons, the Rev. Canon Lloyd Rees. Also present were Gabre-Wold Adams and Emmanuel Foxe. The purpose of this meeting was to inform the Prison Authorities that many Rastafarians were baptised member of the Ethiopian Orthodox Church, and those who were not, are still religious and sincere in their belief. Therefore, they should be allowed to maintain their hairstyle (dreadlocks) as a vital and fundamental part of their faith.

The authorities were also informed that Rastafarians eat no pork, and that their diet was vegetarian. The result of this meeting was a circular instruction 60/1976 to all prison authorities POC/68/313/15/1 24 August 1976 index: The Ethiopian Orthodox Church and Rastafarianism. This document stated that Rastafarianism was not accepted as a valid religion, but the policy of cutting Rastafarian hair in prison would be gradually abandoned.

In Birmingham, Rastafarians who wanted a branch of the Ethiopian Orthodox Church in their community were finding it difficult to secure a building. The Guardian newspaper, Friday 19th November 1976 carried an article titled: *"BUILDING A BRIDGE TO THE YOUNG RASTAFARIANS."* Lindsay Makie reported how a Church of England Vicar was criticised for inviting Rastafarians to use the Church Hall at All Saints, Gravely Hill, Birmingham for the weekly service. A local conservative alleged that the Vicar was encouraging Black militant groups. Father Meedperdas Charles replied that he had the full backing of his congregation and the Church Officials at All Saints. The article was endorsed by two Rasta baptised members of the EOC in London (Deacon Kinfe Gabriel and Tesfa Mariam) who explained the difficulties they were experiencing in Birmingham. Kinfe Gabriel said they were not a political militant group but they were aware of the political significance of a people seeking to establish their cultural identity.

16. Growth of the Movement in Britain

From 1974 onwards, there was a visible growth amongst the Rastafarian communities in Britain. Many journalists and sociologists began to take an interest in the Movement. Various student groups in London and the Midlands began to request the Federation (Local 33) to give lectures on the history and aspirations of the Movement.

The rapid growth of the Movement could also be attributed to a new phenomenon that had developed in Jamaica. By the mid-seventies a new generation of Jamaican musician, who had embraced the Rastafarian faith, had began to project the message through the music. As a result of these developments which coincided with the growth of the Movement in England, Jamaican popular music "reggae" had become synonymous with Rasta (the author will deal with this in a later chapter).

On Saturday 11th January 1975 the first ever Rastafarian conference in England was held at Loyola Hall, Tottenham, London N15. It was organised by the EWF Inc. Local 33 and was attended by many Brethren from all over Britain, including the Twelve Tribes of Israel Organisation, under the local leadership Pepe Judah (Ras Menelik). The conference was chaired by Peter Letang (Mahitima Selassie) and the main speakers were Gabre-Wold Adams, who dealt with the question of centralisation, and Emmanuel Foxe, who emphasised the need for more political awareness within the Movement. One personality present, who was to later emerge in the early 80s, was Jah Bones. The event was published by the West Indian World, 17th January 1975.

In Ethiopia the civil unrest of 1974-75 resulted in the overthrow of the Imperial Ethiopian Government by the

Armed Forces. A letter published in a monthly journal called Africa Magazine, December 1974, from the Rastafarians in Jamaica seem to echo the sentiments of Rastafarians world-wide at the time. It stated:

We the Rastafarian Brethren in Jamaica totally disapprove of the way the Ethiopian Army is treating Emperor Haile Selassie I. Surely the military leaders do not believe that they can sweep away 3,000 years of history and tradition just like that. Whatever wrong the Emperor might have done - and we do not believe that the Elect of God can do any wrong - the army must be careful lest they provoke the wrath of God.

In December 1975 the EWF Inc. Local 33 had mobilised over five hundred Rastafari brethren in support of its first demonstration in sympathy with Haile Selassie I Government. The Brethren and Sistren marched from the HQ building in Portobello Rd. W10 to the Ethiopian Embassy, Princes Gate, London. A petition was handed to the Ethiopian Ambassador on behalf of the Rastafarian community in England and Jamaica and world-wide.

The attempt by the mass-media and the Armed Forces Committee in Ethiopia to discredit the Emperor did not hinder the development of the Movement. On the contrary, the Movement grew more, especially on the international level. However, the relationship between Rastafari and the Ethiopian Orthodox Church became difficult when some priest and deacons omitted the name of the Emperor from certain section of the EOC Liturgy.[1]

Some Brethren who had desired to become active in the Church as priest and deacons were pressured into cutting their locks. As a result of these developments many Rastafari Brethren began to isolate themselves from the

Footnote: [1]Liturgy Book of prayers for the Ethiopian Orthodox Church.

Church. This was happening in America, Jamaica and later in England.

The second and largest of demonstrations by the Rastafarian community in England took place on Saturday 6th March, 1976 and was co-ordinated by N. W. Adams (Jah Blue) and Peter Letang (Mahitima Selassie). Over one thousand Brethren and Sistren from all over Britain participated in this event. The demonstration was called as a response to several incidents of Rastafarians in Jamaica having their locks forcibly cut by the Jamaican Police.

Abba Aregawi Wolde-Gabriel,[1] priest in charge of the EOC in London, blessed the procession at the HQ building in Portobello Road at the start of the journey to Hyde Park via the Jamaican High Commission off Grosvenor Square W1. At the High Commission, a petition was given to the High Commissioner, Mr Arthur Wint,[2] protesting against the gross violation of Rasta Human Rights under article 7 of the Human Rights Charter. The whole event climaxed at Speakers Corner in Hyde Park (London) with Niahbinghi drumming and chanting.

Although this was a unique and historic occasion in the development of the Rastafarian Community in England, it was not covered by the local Black press or any of the national press, even though they were given prior notice through the Press Association. Later on in the year, however, a series of damaging press reports and police harassment were systematically launched against the Movement.

Footnote: [1]Abba Aregawi Wolde Gabriel, now Abuna Yohannes, Bishop of Europe, died in 1997. [2]Mr Arthur Wint died in Jamaica, 1992.

In June 1976 the "Reading Evening Post" printed a story about a *West Indian Mafia Organisation called the "Rastafarians"*. According to the article "Rasta was an institutional crime ring specialising in drugs, prostitution, subversion and blackmail." The story was followed up by the West Indian World with a sensational headline titled *"Rasta Dubbed Mafia"* (July 9-15, 1976). The executive of the EWF Inc. Local 33 made several enquiries into the source of this propaganda but this has remained obscure.

In Birmingham, the West Midlands Police Force commissioned John Brown from the Granfield Institution of Technology to write a report on the situation in Handsworth, regarding Police and Black youths. The Birmingham Post of 8th June 1976 carried an article *"Black Power Movement on the Warpath"*. John Brown's report, "Shades of Grey" (1977) attacked Rasta as "a dangerous criminalised sub-culture."

In September 1976 confrontation between Rastafarians and the authorities came head-on when a Wandsworth County Court Judge granted a Possession Order to the Council for a house at 91 Broomwood Rd, Battersea, London SW11. The house was squatted in by a group of Rastafarians. A similar order by the London Electricity Board (LEB) to disconnect the electricity at 28 St. Agnes Place, Kennington, ended in scuffles between the Brethren and the LEB workmen. The Police, who were present to assist the LEB workmen, arrested six Rastafari Brethren in this incident.

These events were capitalised on by the South London Press, Friday 24th September to 8th October 1976 which featured a three week serial on the Movement titled, *'Rastafari - the Faith of the Black Jews'* by Richard Woolveridge and Jeremy Young. The article was nothing more than sensationalist journalism, aimed at stereotyping people's attitude towards the Rastafarian community, at a time when many parents of Black youths, and the local authorities, including social services, were expressing their anxiety and fears at the growth in the Movement.

Woolveridge said he visited various Rastafarian communities in London and asked who they supported, whether it was the Ethiopian World Federation, Local 33, or the Twelve Tribes of Israel at St. Agnes Place, and their views towards each organisation. In the article of 8th October 1976 under the title *"Rasta HQ UK"*, he said, *"Local 33's approach to religion is considerably different to that of the Twelve Tribes of Israel group... at St. Agnes Place. The brethren from Portobello Rd. do not believe that Haile Selassie I is God, although the Kennington group do."*

How Woolveridge came to this conclusion is very hard to understand. He did visit the building at Portobello Rd. West 10, but the general meeting for that evening was cancelled. Of the seven people he met in the building, five were visitors and only two were members of the Federation. He was told to come back another time when he could meet the executive of the Organisation and was given some leaflets on our aims and objective. Woolveridge did not come back, but he went on to write a lengthy but inaccurate article on what the EWF Inc. Local 33 stood for, and our views on Rasta doctrine.

I am drawing references to this point because other researchers who might genuinely wish to know about the development of the Movement in England can be misguided with information such as this, and will no doubt quote this as fact, as for example, Horace Campbell in his book, **Rasta and Resistance** (1985). On page 188 he writes: *Local 33 of the International EWF, based in Portobello Road, Notting Hill (before it was dispersed and demolished) was, like the neighbourhood from which it emerged, political in orientation* *and did not promote the divinity of the Emperor of Ethiopia, saying: "Selassie is the supreme defender of the Faith of the Ethiopian Orthodox Church. He is not divine, indeed Selassie denied his divinity- but he is worshiped as the spiritual leader of the Movement."*

This quote, presumably from the EWF Inc., Local 33, is totally incorrect whoever or wherever it came from.

In an attempt to redress some of the bad press coverage which the Movement was getting at the time, the Sunday Times featured an article on 3rd October 1976, titled *"Why Black Sect Feels Persecuted"* by Derek Humphrey and Grace Latibeaudiere. The interview was given by the EWF Inc., Local 33 executive, the President of Unit 1 Birmingham, Claudius Haughton, and the President of Unit 2 Leicester, Neville Lane (Wolde Mariam)*. The article dealt with the issues at the time which affected the Rastafarian Community all over Britain, which were the indiscriminate stopping and searching for drugs (herbs) by the Police and general Police harassment. The article went on to quote Commander Robert Bryan, head of Scotland Yard Community Relations Division, who said, "We are teaching our men that everybody who looks like a Rastafarian is not a criminal as this was the attitude of the Police when they confronted members of the Rastafarian Community."

During this period many young Brethren were getting restless within the Movement, saying that more effort should be made towards migrating to Ethiopia/Africa. This was a bone of contention within the Federation's Local 33 and the general Rastafarian Community. Ascento Foxe, who was a dominant personality within the executive of Local 33, always maintained that he was given the

*Footnote: Neville Lane (Wolde Mariam) now lives in South Africa

order from His Majesty's Government to return to Jamaica and help organise the Movement there. Because of this, no real effort was made to meet the needs of these Brethren, and Foxe left for Jamaica shortly after this. However, soon after this, many Brethren left England and migrated to Ethiopia, Ghana and South Africa. Some of the Brethren stayed for a period of time (up to 5 years) before returning to either Jamaica or Britain.

28-34 St Agnes Place, Kennington, London SE11. This building is the hub of Rastafari activities in Britain, Rasta International HQ.

Wolde Mikel (Big Dread) and Wadada, 1976 demonstration. Big Dread now lives in Ghana on the EWF land.

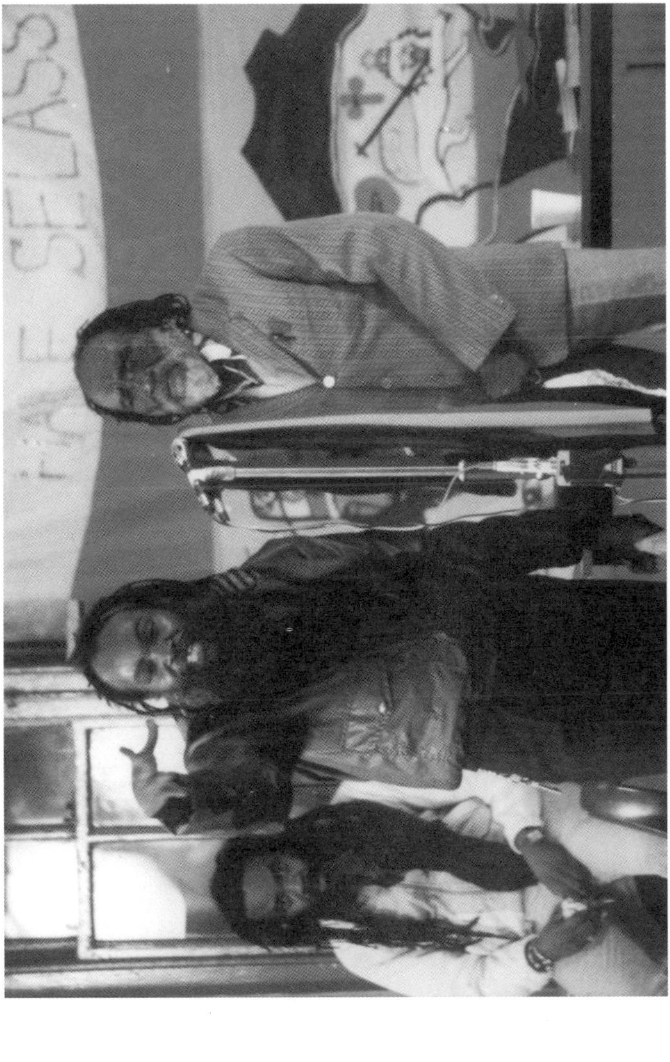

Rastafari gathering at R.U.Z: Left to right, Jah Bones, Bro A. Foxe (Pinto) and Ras Sam Brown.

Rasta Reasoning at Rastafari Universal Zion (R.U.Z.) HQ, Braemar Building, Seven Sisters School, Tottenham, London. Pepe Judah (Menelik) in foreground.

Jah Blue and Bob Marley at No.1 Harrington Gardens, Chelsea, London (1978).

Peace Committee in London: Left to right, C Massop, T Welsh, Bob Marley, and Earl Wadley (1978).

Ethiopian World Federation Incorporated

Proudly Presents

A Grand Rastafarian Ball

to be held at

WOODLAND HALL

CROWN STREET, ACTON, W3

FRIDAY, 22nd SEPTEMBER, '72

From 7 pm until 12 Midnight

Featuing special guest Star

U-ROY backed by the UNDIVIDED

SIR COXSONE bown beat

RICO and his Band

The YOUNG PRINCE

The UNTOUCHABLE

The PEOPLE SOUND

Plus Ethio-Afro West Indian Fashion Show

Tickets 75p in advance at Door £1.

NIAH CURRY GOAT and OILY OILY Refreshments

BUSES 266 206 7, E3 260 88

Tickets from: Ethiopian World Federation Inc., Portobello Road, W10

HAIL RASTA DREAD! DREAD! DREAD!

The first public Rasta Function in London (1972).

Demonstration in London (1976).

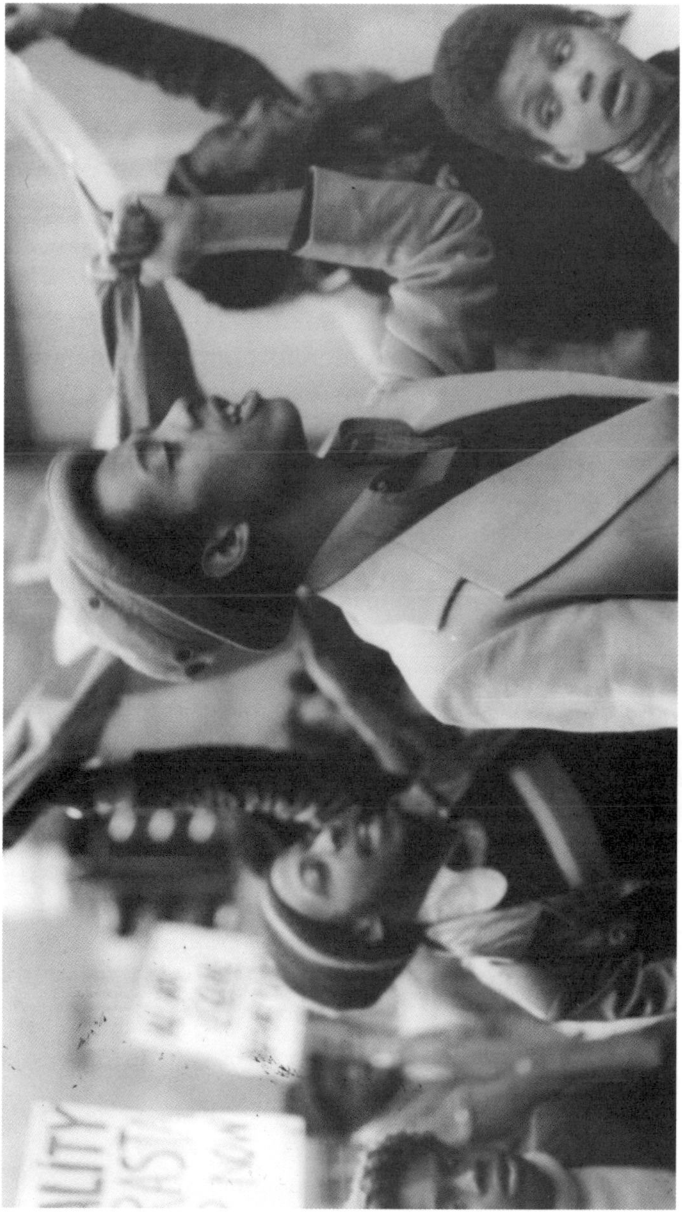

Demonstration in London (1976).

By 1976 onwards the Movement had engulfed a large number of Black youths from all over Britain. Many knew about the Federation and the Ethiopian Orthodox Church, but the overwhelming majority got the message of Jah Rastafari through the lyric of the Jamaican musicians, who had began to use reggae music as a vehicle to chant Rastafari. Those who quickly emerged on the scene were: U-Roy, Burning Spear, the late Peter Tosh, Bunny Wailer and the now legendary Bob Marley.

Born in the Parish of St. Ann, Jamaica (1945-1981), Bob Marley and his music had a tremendous effect on the lives of Black people all over the world who have suffered under the yoke of colonialism and oppression, even as far a field as Australia and New Zealand. His shows in London attracted large numbers of people and it was the same wherever in the world he played.

The hotels where he stayed in London were like a Rasta commune or camp.* There was a continuous gathering of Brethren and Sistren around him. Bob Marley was a deeply committed and sincere Rastafarian. He was honestly concerned about the Movement and contributed substantial sums of money to groups and individuals within the Movement. He was a superstar in his own right, but he never isolated himself from the Rasta Community.

In 1978 he tried to unite the warring political gangs in Kingston, Jamaica. He and several activists were in London before going back to Jamaica to keep the famous Peace Concert there.

*Footnote: "Camp": name for place where Rastafari Brethren met in the early days to reason and debate issues.

This was where he brought the leaders of the two major political parties together, Mr. Edward Seaga and the Prime Minister at the time, Mr Michael Manley.

Three of the political activists on the trip to London with Bob were: Claudius Massop, Earl Wadely (Tek Life) and Anthony Welsh (see Peace Committee photo). This event showed the considerable influence Marley had on current events at the time.

When Bob Marley performed at the Official Zimbabwe Independence Celebrations in April 1980, it was the final accolade of Rastafari Culture reaching across the shores of Jamaica to Africa. Horace Campbell in his book "Rasta and Resistance" said, *"The power of Bob Marley's music has done more to popularise the real issues of the African Liberation Movement than several decades of backbreaking work by Pan-Afrikanists and international revolutionaries." (page 145).*

In 1981 the author was in Jamaica at the time of the solemn occasion of Bob's funeral. It was a great tribute befitting the man. The ceremony was conducted by Archimandrite Abba L. Mandefro of the Ethiopian Orthodox Church. Thousands of people came from all over the world to pay their last respects. People lined the route of the procession from Kingston, deep into the parish of St. Ann where he was laid to rest. For the Rastafarian Community it was the end of an era. The world lost a great musician, but the Rastafarian Community lost a great activist.

The start of the 80s in Britain saw a new Conservative government under Mrs Margaret Thatcher. The new government was almost heralded in with riots in London's inner-cities. In 1980 to 1981, Black youths in Britain took to the streets in open confrontation with the police, and some places were even burnt down. Many Black youths who were sympathizers of the Movement were involved in these sporadic uprising. The result of this was the Lord Scarman Report which emphasises that the Rastafarian faith and aspirations deserved more understanding and sympathy from the British people: "The Brixton Disorders 10-12th April 1981. Report of Inquiry by the Rt Hon Lord Scarman OBE, HMSO Cmnd 8427, page 44, para. 3,106."

More social unrest was to erupt again in 1985 in London and Birmingham. The Broadwater Farm Estate in north London was the setting this time and resulted in the death of one police officer, and three youths being sent to prison.

The new government had been effectively bringing about a lot of changes. However, they all seemed to maintain the status-quo as far as the development of the Black community went. For example, more Black people were going to prison and recent surveys by some Black organisations have shown that Black men in prison outnumber their white counterparts by 14 percent, and Black women by 25 percent.

Homelessness was also on the increase, and the new Immigration Act did not guarantee right of entry for Black people anymore; those who resided in the country most of their lives now have to register as citizens.

But within the Rastafarian Movement two significant changes had come about. These were: more international exchanges between members from different countries and more activities and involvement from Rastafari Sistren. The Greater London Council (GLC) was to later fund various Black organisations, including Rastafarian Organisations which gave many Brethren and Sistren the opportunity to make a more valid contribution towards the wider community.

The GLC policy was condemned by many ministers in Parliament and was later abolished by the government, along with the Inner London Education Authority (ILEA). The riots in 1980-1981 were also to bring about major changes in the attitude of the establishment towards the Rastafarian Community. This was assisted also by the resulting Scarman Report, and various other pressure groups within the society who were now recommending that the Rastafarian Communities should be given official recognition.

17. International Recognition 1980s

The 1980s also saw a new turn of development within the Rastafarian communities in Britain, Canada and Jamaica. There was now an international perspective awareness about the Movement. In Britain on the 23rd July 1981, the second national conference of Rastafari was held at the Brixton Town Hall. The conference was organised by the Brethren and Sistren based at 28 St Agnes Place, Kennington, London SE11, known collectively then as Rasta International. It was attended by five other groups: Tree of Life; Rasta Unity; Mind Soul and Body; Local 33; and Rastafari Universal Zion (RUZ), as well as members from Birmingham (later known as EWF .Local 111), and Rastafarians from all over Britain.

Rasta International emphasised the need for repatriation now, while RUZ emphasised the need for organisation and centralisation before repatriation. This position was seconded by Local 33 and was carried by the majority attending the conference.

On the 12th September, 1981 another meeting was held and the groups all decided they would be centralised under the banner of the then sleeping Ethiopian World Federation, Inc. Ascento Foxe, who was present at the meeting, endorsed the decision as he was the appointed international President of the EWF. Inc. However, although the meeting started out with the best of intentions, it later developed into conflict and division among the Brethren, owing to strong group rivalry. Ato Foxe advised the groups that he would give them their official charter under the EWF's umbrella. Every local of the Ethiopian World Federation, Inc. must have an official charter from the international President and Executive Council which identifies it as a local (a branch).

Several other meetings took place between the different groups until a group in Birmingham, now known as the Ethiopian World Federation, Inc. Local 111, said they had received a charter from an individual in New York, and went on to dispute the authority of Bro. Ascento Foxe as the International President of the Federation.

During these developments Foxe, who was in the process of making contact with the Crown Prince of Ethiopia, His Imperial Highness, Merd Azmatch Asfa Wossen Haile Selassie, decided with his group in west London (Local 33) to ask the Crown Prince for an interview. As a result of the meeting between Ato Foxe and his delegation with the Crown Prince of Ethiopia, the rift was to grow wider between the groups.

The meeting resulted in the Crown Prince adding the word "Imperial" to the name of the Federation, e.g. Imperial Ethiopian World Federation, Inc.* He also gave Foxe a letter endorsing his action, and stated clearly that he the Crown Prince would resume the role of his Father The Emperor, as trustee of the I.E.W.F. Inc.

The other groups involved said they were not consulted or invited to have representatives on the delegation which met the Crown Prince, and therefore could not support or accept any decision or agreement which Bro. Ascento Foxe came back and proposed.

The whole affair later became public knowledge and was carried in the "Voice" newspaper in two articles: "RASTAFARIAN RIFT WIDENS" 4th May 1985 (by Tony Sewell) and "TALKBACK" 25th May 1985. Jah Bones of Rastafari Universal Zion went on to launch a bitter attack against

*Footnote: Local 33 was dissolved in 1983 and was later known as the Imperial Ethiopian World Federation, Inc.

Foxe and the "Imperial House." This dispute has not been resolved and has caused the groups involved to isolate themselves from each other.

The EWF Inc. Research and Repatriation Committee,* based at 28 St. Agnes Place, did not get involved in the public squabble but they also hit the headlines in the local Black press.

"The Voice" reported that in 1985 they had collected over seven thousand pounds (£7,000) to bring a young girl, Colleen Reid, from Ethiopia for a life saving heart operation. Her father, a Rastafarian, lived on the Land Shashamane. Their effort was a complete success and the group later decided to continue to work towards improving the hospital facilities at Shashamane, or building a new and larger hospital.

While the organisation was involved in these fund raising activities, to meet their objective, one of their members Seymour McLean was charged at Southwark Crown Court for stealing over 1,000 books from the British Museum, The School of Oriental and African Studies, The Foreign Office Library and the Bible Society. They were worth eight thousand pounds (£8,000). Ras Seymour said that it was his mission to *"liberate" Ethiopian history books from the British Museum and other libraries.*

The three week trial ended with Ras Seymour McLean being sentenced to nine months imprisonment. He was accused with three others, Mrs Monica Grant, Mr Phillip Taylor (Ras Binghi) and Mr Roach, who were all acquitted on charges of handling, apart from Mr Roach who was

*Footnote: After the 1981 conference at Brixton Town Hall, the Research and Repatriation Committee functioned as EWF at 28 St Agnes Place, Kennington, London.

given a 6 month suspended sentence. Before entering court that morning, Ras Seymour said: *"The case is about the freedom of the Magdala Collection, which was stolen by the British from Ethiopia in 1868. The youths must know the truth about their past."* In his defence, Barrister Berry Bryan stated that McLean's motive was never dishonest, he was on a mission to recover what rightfully belongs to Black people. Stephen Bell, a researcher and expert in Ethiopian history, who was called by McLean's Defence, told the court that the British Museum holds the stolen treasures of the Magdala Collection which is a record of Ethiopia's ancient history. Although Bro. Seymour McLean went to prison, he was regarded as a hero by many Rastafari Brethren and Sistren for his effort.

The Magdala Collection comprises a number of priceless manuscripts, gold and silver crosses, church icons and many other priceless jewels that were stolen when Sir Robert Napier, under Queen Victoria, invaded Ethiopia and challenged Emperor Theodore. Theodore, realising he would be defeated, committed suicide. His court was looted by the British soldiers who stole everything in sight. This history was corroborated in the article" Ethiopia Fight for it's Lost Heritage" (African Events 1985 by Dr Richard Pankhurst).

Two important documents dealing with the Movement in England were published in 1982. One was by the Catholic Commission For Racial Justice and the other was by the Greater London Council's Ethnic Minorities Committee. In its summary, The Catholic Commission for Racial Justice's "Notes and Reports No.10: Rastafarians in Jamaica and Britain", concluded that:
"Rastafarianism should be recognised as a valid religion, and the members and leaders of other religious groups should attempt to engage the proponents of Rastafarianism in dialogue..."

"Christians and Christian churches should take whatever opportunities they may have or be able to create to relate to Rastafarians as they would to the believers of other non-Christian faiths. For instance, Rastafarians often lack places to meet; and Christian churches could consider allowing Rastafarians use of their premises.

The Christian churches and other religious groups should exercise appropriate influence over their own institutions (for example schools, children's homes, etc.) so that they may relate to the members of the Rastafarian movement with true knowledge and sound understanding, rather than with an attitude born of fear, ignorance and prejudice.

Rastafarian styles of dress (e.g. locks and head-dress) should be accepted as authentic religious expressions and legitimate cultural forms.

The Home Office should use its influence to ensure that penal institutions have a regard to these legitimate forms. We welcome the initiative of the Home Office in revising Circular 60/1976 and their reported intention to instruct governors of penal institutions not to forcibly cut off the Rastafarian locks. We would further suggest that, in principle, Rastafarians in penal institutions should be allowed the same privileges as are accorded to other religious believers.

All authority figures should scrupulously avoid any form of harassment or discrimination against Rastafarians. It is especially important that professional workers such as teachers, social workers, police, prison and probation officers should be sensitive to the tendency to stereotype black people in general and Rastafarians in particular.

Social and community work agencies should take positive steps to serve a multiracial, multi-cultural society and in so doing, recognise the importance of learning from and correctly repre-

senting the variety of culturally based views and practices. Rastafarians should be in a genuine position of not only obtaining effective help, but also giving it."

These seven recommendations were welcomed by members of the Rastafarian community not only in Britain, but also in Jamaica where it was carried by a national paper "The Star". In June 1982, Lord Elton replied to Lord Avebury in the House of Lords that "the Home Office is considering whether Rastafari should be recognised as a valid religion and that Rastafarians in penal institutions should be allowed the same privileges as are accorded to other religious believers."

The second document of importance to Rastafari in England came at the end of 1982. In July 1982 the Greater London Council Ethnic Minorities Committee decided to fund a Rastafarian Organisation, RUZ. A report was prepared in December to provide the committee with information about Rastafarians generally and as a basis for considering policies in relation to the Movement, which includes funding of Rastafarian groups. The GLC's Ethnic Minorities Committee Report (6-12-82) by the Director General, titled "Rastafarianism in Greater London", was the result.

The findings of the study suggest that there were specific practical steps that could be taken by the Council and other London local authorities, in regards to Rastafari. They suggested that:

Many individual Rastafarian groups are preparing community development projects, such as youth schemes, mother and toddler groups, social clubs, employment, educational and training schemes and the publication of information booklets on Rastafari.

They need practical... support in developing these projects. They also need assistance in finding suitable buildings in which to locate schemes.

The Home Office should be asked to consider their policy towards Rastafarianism as a religion, in relation not only to prisons, but also borstals and detention centres.

There is a need for accommodation for young adult Rastafarians who have left home. How this should be provided should be investigated and discussed with Rastafari groups and existing bodies providing hostels.

Rastafarians are extremely involved in their own history. A full account of their history in Britain is still to be written. Some Rastas have spoken about their desire to establish an archive. It would provide a valuable service both to Rastafarians and, as an aid to understanding the movement, to the wider community. This is an aspect which could be pursued with the Rastafarian community as part of the Committee's consultation programme.

The report's recommendations concluded:

That officers report again, following further consultation with Rastafarian groups and other appropriate organisations on a programme for their community.

That the Committee agree in principle to give priority in their 1983-84 budget to funding suitable projects, as in above, to promote the welfare of the Rastafarian community in London.

That representation be made to the Home Secretary asking him to extend his consideration of Rastafarianism as a religion to including borstals and detention centres, as well as prisons.

That this report be referred to the Single Homeless Sub-Committee with the recommendation that they give special attention to the issue of accommodation referred to in paragraph... above.

Some of these recommendations have been met and several Rastafarian groups have received funding, notable among these are: Rastafari Universal Zion (RUZ), Rastafarian Advisory Service (RAS), Tree of Life, and the Ethiopian World Federation Inc, Local 33 now known as the Imperial Ethiopian World Federation Inc. (Asfa Wossen Local 1). Many other groups also received funding, some for business projects also.

In Canada the Rastafarian community, who were experiencing the same kind of social and economic oppression to I and I in Britain, were also organising amongst themselves. They hosted their first international conference on the 23rd July - July 25th 1982. The theme of the conference was "The family is the strength of the nation" and was coordinated by Sister Charmaine Montague and Brother Terence "Chico" Paul. The conference was attended by Brethren and Sistren from all over the Caribbean and various issues which affected the Movement were discussed through four workshops, which were:

(1) Repatriation
Haile Selassie I Conception
Diet / Alcohol / Smoking

(2) Rastafari, the Black Community and Society at large
Interaction between Rastafarian and non-Rastafarian
Rastafari as a viable alternative for Black Youths
The Law / Police / Media Conception of I and I

(3) Rastafari and the Family
Family Structure
Women's role within the family and the Movement

(4) Models for children, e.g. locks etc.

Rastafari and education within the political and economic system
What constitutes education
Should Rastafarians be involved in politics e.g. voting

All of these issues generated a lot of discussion and at times some heated debates, but none more so than workshop No.3. Rastafari and the Family.

Recommendations - Workshop No.1.

In Workshop No.1. there was a general consensus about the development of the Movement. Rastafarians' Socio-Cultural lifestyle consists of their way of dressing, the food they eat, known as Ital, the dreadlocks appearance and their whole philosophy and way of life (their livity). It concluded that Rastafarians have the same beliefs regardless of the country they reside in.

The family that prays together, giving chants and praises to Jah-Rastafari, stays together. There is a need for more collective reasoning on the teachings and livity of Rastafari. This should be done so that I and I will have the same common principles, but still be able to retain I and I individuality.

Recommendations - Workshop No.2.

There should be a better understanding between the Rastafarian Community and the Community at large. Because of this misconception perpetrated by the various institutions, Rastafarians should establish their own means of communication e.g. newspapers, videos, books, reasoning sessions, music and art. Because of the significance of Ganja (Herbs) or the wisdom weed, this should be decriminalised the world over.

Rastafari as a way of life is a viable alternative to the western acculturation presented to Black youths. There should be formalised reasoning sessions to expose youths to Rastafari way of life, e.g. seminars in schools, community centres, etc.

Workshop No.3 did not make any clear recommendations, but dealt in depth with various issues that related to the Rastafarian family. The word 'family' was defined and its relation to different cultures, also the role of different members of the family, was discussed. Some Sistrens pointed out that they did not want just "equality", but a chance to let their voices be heard and listened to. It was felt that Brethren should give Sistrens equal chances of opportunity and support.

Another burning issue raised was that of polygamy. While several Brethren supported this view, most Sistren were not for the idea and did not support it. A compromise was reached whereby if Sistrens favour a polygamous setting, that is fine as long as they are in total agreement with this way of life and it is not forced upon them.

The kind of role model that should be set for Rastafarian children were some of the questions raised by members of the conference. Should Rastafarian parents locks their children's hair or wait until they are old enough to choose their own lifestyle?

It is well known that Rastafarian children are constantly ridiculed both by the administration and their peers.

Workshop No.4. dealt with the issue of education and political activities within the Movement. Should the Movement be involved in formal political activity such as voting or running for office?

Recommendations - Workshop No.4.

Rastafarians should seek for their economic independence. There is a need for a strong economic base. This can be done through co-operatives and international trade. Although our people are scattered all over the world, the majority live in Africa and the Caribbean, therefore political involvement in these regions is a necessity. "Government is not infallible, they are not without going wrong. Government is only an executive control, a centralised authority for the purpose of expressing the will of the people. Before you have a government you must have people. Without people there can be no government. The government must be therefore an expression of the will of the people." (Marcus Garvey). "Where there is no vision, the people perish: but in the multitude of counsellors there is safety." (Proverbs Chap. 11, Verse 14).

The three day conference was completed on Sunday 25th July with a cultural show. All the delegates that attended the conference thought it was successful and enlightening. The countries represented at the conference were: Jamaica, St. Kitts, St. Lucia, Dominica, Monsterrat, St. Thomas (U.S. Virgin Island); American cities, New York City, California, Detroit and Nebraska, and Canadian cities: Ottawa, Hamilton, Winnepeg and Kitchener. The delegates decided they would attend Jamaica the following year for the Second Annual Rastafari International Theocratic Conference.

Conference '83 Jamaica

The second annual conference entitled Rastafari International Theocratic Assembly was held at the University College of the West Indies, Mona Campus, Kingston, Jamaica. It was scheduled to run from 18th - 25th July '83 but this was extended for one day to finalise all deliberations.

The conference was attended by delegates from the Caribbean, America and Europe, and the Science Auditorium at Mona Campus was filled to its capacity. The Green, Gold and Red was in evidence everywhere, and Herbs (Marijuana) was smoked freely throughout all sessions.

The first day was taken up with introducing delegates, while greetings and solidarity messages poured in from Rastafarian communities worldwide. Many important issues were discussed and repatriation became the focal point of discussion on the second day. The delegations spent four days touring various Rastafari "Mansions" of foundation throughout Jamaica. This started with Prince Emmanuel's camp at Bull Bay. They also visited Ras Daniel of Trelawny and Bongo U of Mo'bay, also Ras Macdonald on the Triple I Food Project. On returning to Mona on Monday 25th July, a special concert was given by sister Rita Marley, performing with Ethiopian reggae group "Dallol". The Wailers also performed along with Ziggy Marley.

Ras Bonerges and Ras Bongo Time gave the conference their full support as elders within the Movement. On Tuesday 26th July the final summing up and a final draft and conclusion were prepared for all delegates. Everyone agreed the conference was a total success.

Rastafari International Theocracy Assembly

July 18-26 Jamaica U.W.I.
Summary Resolutions

Having examined the resolutions/proposals emerging from the reasoning and discussion within the conference, the following four (4) categories were predominant:

Spiritual/Cultural,
Health & Education,
Administration,
Fund-Raising and Economic.

In addition, meaningful priority was given to the discussion on Dawtas and Youth, Media & Communication, Human Rights and Collective Security. The following are the Resolutions covering these areas.

Spiritual/Cultural

Repatriation was the principle focus for both Spiritual and Cultural. The Rastafari International Divine Order of the Nyahbingi should be the responsible source to provide spiritual guidance regarding Rastafari Religious Foundation and Livitical Authority.

Health & Education

Education and health pursued in a balanced motive are consistent with His Majesty's teachings, with divine laws and with natural functions. Therefore, technical, religious and practical education should be encouraged to promote effective cultural livity and I-vine spiritual groundation.

Administration

The administration of the Rastafari Community should be handled at two distinct levels: a Rastafari International Secretariat and a Rastafari International Theocracy Government (functional).

Media & Communication

An independent Rastafari International Media Communication Centre should be developed to monitor Rastafari International Affairs, Information and Community News Release.

Daughters & Youths

Youths and Sistrens should be given greater freedom and assistance to develop responsible economic, educational, and family life programmes appropriate to their organisation and functions/roles (critical to service their social, health and nutritional needs).

Repatriation

A special Repatriation Committee should be instituted immediately within the Rastafari International Secretarial, to develop the repatriation exercise and to implement formal agreements relative to African states and the O.A.U.

Human Rights / Collective Security

That each regional secretariat be responsible to develop an organ to liaise with regional governments and service institutions in each respective territory, to lobby for and secure the collective civil rights of Rastafari individuals and groups.

Fund-Raising / Economic

That fund-raising for repatriation and related administrative services of the international secretariat be centred around cultural shows, retail of books, lectures, films / videos, Rastafari festivals, arts & crafts and the sale of collective teachings of the Rastafari elders.

Rastafari Focus '86

On 14th-27th July 1986, an international gathering of the Rastafarian Community took place in England. The event was held at the Commonwealth Institute in London, and had as its theme: "Word, Sound and Power". Many delegates came from the U.S.A, Canada and the Caribbean, along with Brethren and Sistren from England.

This was not a conference, but a cultural gathering where Brethren and Sistren came together to exchange ideas and strengthen each other in carrying forward the works and development of the Movement.

The 14 day event was opened with a prayer and followed by drumming and chanting by the Elder Ras Boanerges ("Sons of Thunder") and his Angels Ras Ivor (Ras Ivi) and Ras Iville from the Nyahbingi House. The Master of Ceremony, Mahitima Selassie then briefly outlined the aims of Rastafari Focus '86, thus:

The *history of Rastafari has gone through many stages of development. It has suffered many setbacks, it has suffered persecution through the Babylonian system, individually as well as on a collective basis. This is why for the next 14 days through Rastafari Focus the message of our experiences will be delivered to all who attend these reasonings."*

Following this statement, a song was dedicated to the Brethren and Sistren of South Africa, calling for the Liberation of all Black people universally.

Black Liberation Day (repeat)
Oh what a great day that must be, when Africa is free
No more Apartheid, no more genocide
Oh what a great day that must be, when Africa is free

It was the first time many leading Brethren from the Nyahbinghi House in Jamaica had attended a gathering in England, most notable of whom was Ras Boanerges founder of the "Youth Black Faith" in Jamaica of the 1940s. Some of these Brethren who made presentations were Ras Michael A. Lorne - Attorney at Law; Ras Historian - founder of the Rastafari Movement Association (RMA); Ras Cover, and the two Brethren Ras Ivor (now Ras Ivi) and Bro. Iville who are known for the sweet and melodic power which they express on the nyahbinghi harps (drums). Many other Brethren and Sistren from other parts of the Caribbean and the U.K. also made presentations.

The whole event was well organised, for which full credit must be given to Sistren Liveth Ivory of the Rastafari Advisory Service (R.A.S).

Ras Boanerges (Bongo Watto) Speaks

"Africa is the foundation of the world, the first embryonic place upon the face of creation that man could exist. I took up my banner in 1947 and started to go about the street following the footsteps of my brother, footsteps of the Honourable Marcus Garvey. I have studied Marcus Garvey's philosophy, and saw it was the true light unto Black people. He was one of the first prophets of Jamaica that enlighten the people morally towards Africa, to bring the people to the standard and the knowledge that Africa was our ancient foundation and what brutality we

have suffered that has cause us to be in Jamaica and scattered over the four wing of the earth. So Marcus Garvey suffered a great deal. We the Rastafarians have come to declare the policies of H.I.M Haile Selassie I.
Five of our Brethren took up their banner along with their knowledge of the Bible and turned onto the streets, realising what the situation was/is among our people and the spirit of truth really written upon us. As youth we called ourselves "Youth Black Faith" because in the early days we used to receive pamphlets about Ethiopia from Sylvia Pankhurst, an English woman who use to be a right hand to His Majesty's Palace. Those pamphlets were received every month in the years 1945-46. Each of the pamphlets was printed with the words "Ethiopia Black International" so this explains how we got the name "Youth Black Faith."

During those periods on the streets we suffered police brutality and imprisonment. In those early days you could not wear red, gold and green buttons. The flag had to be wrapped very neatly so that no one could see it. If a man wore locks on his head he was scorned, no one respected him, no one looked on him. Those whom you were acquainted with put you aside instantly.

Now concerning the position as regards the Faith and Administration coming through the ages. We have got Brethren who took up the struggle through the Ethiopian World Federation, who toiled for this cause. But the majority of the strains, stress and anxiety fell upon the dreadlocks Rastafarian. Now today we see that the dreads, dreadlocks brothers, are spread over the earth by the power of the Almighty. We have to give HIM thanks and praise. Remember the teaching of prophecy which is a scroll. I am bidding all Brethren and Sistren who take up these footsteps - don't leave this until when we reach the river Euphrates, then you can bind it and cast it off into the river Euphrates and say, down with Babylon, who rose up against Ethiopia." (extracts: Ras Boanerges Rastafari Focus 1986. Published by R.A.S.).

The international gathering has been a regular feature of the Movement since the eighties and has served to consolidate the Rastafari Community even stronger. This has led to much internal co-operation, and sharing of information on issues that affect each group, in different countries. This gathering was a complete success in that many Brethren and Sistren from America, the Caribbean and Europe were now meeting on a regular basis and discussing the various issues that affect the Rastafari Movement world-wide.

It could be said that by the end of the 80s the Rastafarian Movement had gained a high degree of international recognition. In the United States of America, a High Court in New York ruled that dreadlocks, Rastafarian hairstyle, is protected under the constitution of America. As a result of this ruling, the court said that no member of the Movement should have their locks cut by prison officials.

This unanimous 7-0 decision was taken in the case of Jamaican 32 year old Alfredo Lewis by the Court of Appeal in the State of New York. In the opinion of the court, Lewis was sincere in his beliefs and to cut his locks would infringe on those beliefs and his constitutional rights. ('Caribbean Times', 21st November 1986).

In Britain, Trevor Dawkins, a Rastafarian, contested that he was illegally discriminated against when an employee of the government's inter-departmental car service refused to employ him, if he did not cut his locks. Ras Trevor Dawkins' application for a job as driver with the government's transport service, within the Crown Suppliers, was rejected when he told his interviewer, Ms Barbara Herbert, the Senior Section Leader at the Department of Environment, that he would not consider cutting his locks for the job.

After a ten week hearing, the London South Industrial Tribunal, by a 2-1 majority decision, decided that Rastafarians are an ethnic group protected by the Race Relations Act 1976. (C.R.E. press release 31st March 1989). The ruling, which takes its precedence from the House of Lords decision concerning Sikhs, found that Rastafarians met the criteria of an ethnic group. Although the decision is by no means binding in other courts, its record on the statutes book means that there is precedence if a matter of this nature should arise again.

The main evidence on Rastafari nationalism came from Dr. E. Cashmore who is regarded by the establishment as an expert on the subject. Many Brethren and Sistren welcomed the decision. Ras Kefentse Tskani of The Ethiopian World Federation, Research and Repatriation Committee said, *"This case is a great victory, not just for Ras Trevor, but for all Rastafarians in Britain."*

These developments within the Movement outside Jamaica have been very significant, especially in Britain when one considers the short space of time the Movement has established itself in this country. The end of the 80s in Britain has left the Rastafarian community with a strong infrastructure for further development into the 90s and beyond.

There has been significant and fundamental development since the inception of the Movement in Britain in the late 30s. However all efforts to centralise the Movement in an effective single unified body has still eluded the Movement.

Some groups such as The Rastafarian Advisory Service (R.A.S.), Rastafari Universal Zion (R.U.Z.) and the Ethiopian World Federation, Inc. have fulfilled the needs of their members as a base for support, and self-development for their everyday struggle within the wider society.

The Research and Repatriation Committee* and the Ethiopian World Federation, Inc. Local 111, Birmingham group have worked mostly on a programme of repatriation. These groups have given financial help to the early pioneer Brethren and their families who live on The Land in Ethiopia, and are working towards migrating to live in Ethiopia themselves. Other Rastafari Brethren, through their own efforts, are also living in Ghana and Zimbabwe.

*Footnote: The Research and Repatriation Committee of the EWF is now known as the Negusa Negast Local 3, branch.

18. Repatriation

Fear not; For I am with thee. I will bring thy seed from the East and gather thee from the West. I will say to the North, Give up; and to the South, Keep not back. Bring my sons from afar, and my daughters from the ends of the earth, even everyone that is called by my name; for I have created him for my glory.
Isaiah 43 v 5-7.

Apart from the belief in the divinity of H.I.M. Emperor Haile Selassie I as the true and living God, repatriation is the other pillar within the doctrine of the Rastafari Movement, and is therefore one of the most sensitive and emotive of issues within the Movement. "We cannot give up a continent for an island." (Rastafari saying).

Ever since Black people were forcibly removed from Africa and were brought to the West to build western economies, it was the aspiration of many Blacks to return to their ancestral homeland, Africa. In the 1920s our beloved prophet Marcus Garvey, through his organisation the U.N.I.A, developed the Back to Africa doctrine, and his shipping company, named the "Black Star Liner". However, his efforts were sabotaged by the U.S Government, and since then, the torch of repatriation has been maintained within the concept of the Rastafarian Movement.

In 1959 the Rev. Claudius Henry, functioning under his organisation called "The Seventh Emmanuel Brethren", made repatriation the main policy of his organisation. They distributed over fifteen thousand tickets at one shilling each in Jamaica to the people who were willing to migrate to Africa. Many ordinary Jamaicans and members of the Rastafarian Community sold their personal belongings in the hope of returning to Africa, but this never materialised.

In 1961 the then Prime Minister of Jamaica, the late Norman W. Manley, endorsed a project for Rastafarians and other Back-to-Africa groups in Jamaica to visit several African states on a feasibility Mission. The mission was to specifically study the feasibility of Repatriation to Africa. (See Mission to Africa Report).

The Mission received a positive response from all the countries they had visited. However when the Mission returned to Jamaica, the leading Brethren with the Rastafarian communities failed to take the initiative and organise effectively amongst themselves.

In the late 60s and early 70s, after much trials and tribulation, The Ethiopian World Federation, Inc. Shashamane Land Grant Development & Resettlement Committee was established in Central Village, St. Catherine, Jamaica. It comprised of membership from three locals of the Federation, Locals 43, 25 and Local 77.

After a lot of hard work and a lot of setbacks, a settlement on the original Shashemane land grant in Ethiopia was finally achieved, under the sponsorship of Local 43. Repeated representations were made to the Minister of the Imperial Court of Ethiopia by Bro. Solomon Wolfe, President of Local 43, and other Brethren living on the land. As a result of this, a Committee of high ranking ministers within the Government of Ethiopia held a meeting on the 30th June 1968 at the Grand Palace, under the chairmanship of the Minister of the Imperial Court of Ethiopia.

On this occasion the Committee deliberated and decided that each family on the land should be given two point two (2.2) hectares* (5 acres) of land. As a follow up on

*Footnote: 1 hectare = 2.5 acres. There is now a H.Q. building on the land Shashamane, Ethiopia.

this decision, on August 13th, 1968 a total of three gashas (300 acres) of land for twelve persons were officially given over by the Administrative Secretary General and Surveyor of the local Ethiopian administration. The names of the twelve recipients were: Solomon Wolfe, Gerald Brissett, Desmond Christie, Clifton Baugh, Carmen Clarke, Noel Dyer, Gladstone Robinson, Vincent Beckford, Zepha Malcolm, Landford Baugh, Uriah Brown and Willie Hillman. Ten of the settlers were Jamaican and two were Americans.

After receiving the plots of land, the twelve settlers formed a committee, the Pioneer Settlers Corps (PSC), and elected seven officers to manage the committee affairs. The immediate responsibility of the committee was to set up an effective administration on the land, to foster a spirit of brotherhood and to create means by which the land could be mechanically cultivated. The committee also pledged to work in close cooperation with the Imperial Ethiopian Government, in all planning and development.

In Jamaica the Resettlement Committee of the E.W.F. Inc. made representation to the Jamaican Government under Mr Michael Manley, Prime Minister and son of the late N. W. Manley, for aid towards the land in Ethiopia. The delegation was led by Bro. Wilfred Redwood along with eight other Brethren. They visited the office of Senator Dudley Thompson and discussed the programme they had to develop the land in Ethiopia. They also told Senator Thompson that it would take at least $100 million Ethiopian dollars to help develop and settle other Brethren and their families on the land.

The senator promised the delegation that a full report would be given to the Prime Minister. Letters asking for economic assistance were also sent to the United Nations Economic Commission for Latin America, and all relevant institutions and governmental bodies which the Brethren thought necessary, including the United States Government.

The Prime Minister, Mr Michael Manley, after getting a full report on the development of the land in Ethiopia, said he was willing to aid the programme. However, by 1974 a disagreement developed between Bro. Wilfred Redwood, president of Local 25 of the E.W.F. Inc., and other Brethren of the Resettlement Committee, and by the end of 1976 a lot of hard work and effort was frustrated yet again. The revolution in Ethiopia also played its part in disrupting the land grant programme in Ethiopia. Some Brethren have left Ethiopia for Kenya and others had returned to Jamaica since then. Some Brethren also felt they could not work with the Marxist regime as they were responsible for the overthrow of the Imperial Ethiopian Government. Since then the development of the land, given to us by His Majesty, has again come to a stand-still, except for those Brethren from EWF Inc. at 28 St. Agnes Place, London SE11, who had begun to support the Brethren living on the land, and also the Ethiopian World Federation Local 111, in Birmingham.

The EWF members in London have worked towards finishing a building begun by Bro Christie and Brethren on the land. This building now serves as headquarters of the Ethiopian World Federation, Inc. in Ethiopia. Additional structures are in progress but need support from the wider Rasta Community.

By the end of the 80s and early 90s, the Movement had levelled out in Britain. Most groups in their respective communities were involved in their own programmes. The absence of Ascento Foxe (Bro. Pinto), who was now living between the U.S and Jamaica, could also be said to leave a vacuum within the Movement in London. While many Brethren may not have agreed with him most of the time, he did stimulate discussion on certain important issues that affected the Movement. The Imperial Ethiopian World Federation, Inc., which he is responsible for developing, has not reached the general Rastafarian Community in England and the membership has hardly any dialogue with the rest of the Rastafarian Community. However, Bro. Ascento Foxe is still very active in Jamaica and America, as head of the Haile Selassie I Church. The doctrine of this church is similar to the Ethiopian Orthodox Church, the difference being all praises is to His Majesty Emperor Haile Selassie as God. It is represented in London in the Harlesden area.

Year of the Creator

In 1992 a small group of Brethren and Sistren were meeting at the offices of the Rastafari Advisory Service, London W6. The group called themselves the Centenary Committee and their aim was to organise a trip to Ethiopia, to celebrate the 100th year, the Centenary of His Imperial Majesty Emperor Haile Selassie I. Information was sent out to all the different groups within the Rastafarian Community, both national and international. The response to this programme was very good, although many Brethren and Sistren were slow to come forward and participate. The Brethren and Sistren who made up the Centenary Committee were Bro. Peter, Ras Shango, Ras M, Sis Liveth, Ras Clan, Sis. Benji, and Jah Blue (the author) who became part of the committee in the early '92. Although this body was responsible for co-ordinating the trod to Ethiopia, other Brethren and Sistren made valuable contributions to the programme, such as Sis Sheba, Sis. Deborah, Ras Pablove and Ras Tagassa (EWF Inc, Development Officer) in Ethiopia.

The aims and objectives of the Centenary Committee were as follows:

* To recognise and celebrate the 100th anniversary of H.I.M. Emperor Haile Selassie I on earth.

* To gather internationally and to celebrate the unity of Rastafarians worldwide.

* To encourage world governments to honour and pay tribute to the Personage of H.I.M. Haile Selassie I of Ethiopia, who is recognised by all as the leading Statesman of the century.

* To mark the realisation of the repatriation Movement.

*To create and encourage business enterprise in Shashamane, Ethiopia. This initiative will also aim to stimulate the growth of business enterprises in other African states.

* To promote "The Year of the Creator" wherever humanly possible.

* To link with all fraternal organisations who share these aims and objectives.

Part of the programme of the Centenary Committee (C.C.) was to invite a delegation of elders from the Nyahbingi House in Jamaica, to take part in this historic celebration. They were Bongo Rocky, Empress Baby-I, Ras Ivi, Ma Ashanti, Sis Faye and Bongo Solo.

The Centenary Committee launched its programme for 1992, The Year of the Creator, at the Hammersmith Town Hall (London W6) on Friday 28th February. Over 300 Brethren and Sistren attended the event, including Abba Selassie of the Ethiopian Orthodox Church and other Municipal leaders, along with the press.

The launch was a complete success and started a series of tours by the Committee to various Rastafarian Communities in the Midlands of England, outlining the programme of the Centenary's trod to Ethiopia. The events culminated in a memorable farewell reception at the One Love Children Centre, Brixton SW9 on the 26th June 1992. It was a truly moving and spiritual gathering.

On the 28th June, 1992 over 100 Rastafari Brethren and Sistren departed from Heathrow Airport for Ethiopia. In Ethiopia the Rastafarian Community was warmly received by the Ethiopian people. The opening scheduled for the Centenary delegation was a concert at the National Theatre, Addis Ababa. Over one thousand Ethiopians attended the event.

The international delegation to Ethiopia in 1992 was historic and visits around the country were met by crowds of Ethiopians wherever the delegation went. On the 23rd July celebrations were held on the land Shashamane. A more detailed account of the trip to Ethiopia is documented in a booklet entitled "Centenary Trod To Ethiopia" by Ras Ivi; also the official video by the Centenary Committee. The Centenary Committee took the responsibility to co-ordinate the building of the Tabernacle on the land of Shashamane.

Since the visit to Ethiopia, there is a strong mood of optimism within the Rastafarian Community in England. Not surprisingly the call for unity is much stronger and, for the first time in Britain, the Rastafarian Community is co-operating more than ever before. Another positive move forward from the visit to Ethiopia was contact between the delegation and representatives of the Organisation of African Unity (O.A.U.) at the headquarters in Addis Ababa on the 4th August 1992. As a result of this historic and significant meeting, the O.A.U. requested a position paper on repatriation from the Rastafarian Community.

The Centenary of H.I.M. was celebrated worldwide by the Rastafarian communities. In Jamaica a tour around the 14 parishes was programmed by the Nyahbinghi House. Bunny Wailer is said to have made valuable contributions in these efforts and the celebration was well received by the Jamaican community.

After nearly four decades the Movement is now firmly established in England. It has played a major role in helping to raise the level of consciousness of many Black people in Britain. It is also a known fact that Britain has the second largest Rastafarian Community outside of Jamaica, and is very influential within the Rasta Community worldwide.

The trip to Ethiopia has also intensified the mood for repatriation and major developments are now under way to continue and strengthen the link with the Motherland, Ethiopia-Africa.

19. Brief Summary of the Movement

Since the early infancy in the growth of the Movement in England, there has been many significant and dramatic changes, not only in Britain, but on the world stage. For one thing, Russia, the bastion of world communism, has fallen, taking all the eastern block countries with her. In Ethiopia, Mengistu's Communist regime which overthrew the Imperial Government has also fallen apart, with his departure to Zimbabwe. In South Africa the white racist regime has sued for peace and Nelson Mandela become President elect of the country. His party, the African National Congress (ANC) was swept to power through the democratic process in 1994.

Since the historic trod to Ethiopia for His Majesty's Centenary Celebrations in 1992, there has been an upsurge of activities within the Rastafari Community. Several Brethren from the Nyahbinghi House have visited London; Ras Irie Lion, Bongo Time, and Ras Boanerges for the second time, along with Ras Ibo.

The EWF Inc. has also seen an upsurge in development since 1992. This started out with a series of International Presidents' meetings leading up to an interim International ad hoc committee who then organised the 57th annual convention of the EWF Inc., in New York from the 10th to the 18th July 1995. This meeting was the first international convention for over twenty-five years and is a tremendous and historic achievement which can only strengthen the development of the EWF Inc. world-wide.

The mood and desire for repatriation still burn deeply and how this is eventually resolved, no one can say for sure. However, one thing is certain, more Rastafari brethren and sistren are making their own way home to Ethiopia / Africa, our ancestral Homeland.

Within the Rastafari Movement in England there is a strong infrastructure, although each group is working on their own programme. Everyone realise the need for the Movement to centralise as I and I progress through the 21st century and beyond. I hope the information contained in this book will help I and I to reflect, examine and analyse the works that have taken place over the last four decades, and to framework them into our march to the future.

> *"From Cape to Cairo, Africa must be free."*
> (Rastafarian saying).

20. Characteristics of Rastafari and its Organisations

From the early development of the Movement in Jamaica, the three founding fathers of the Movement all had their own following. All were members of Marcus Garvey's Organisation, the Universal Negro Improvement Association (U.N.I.A.). Archibald Dunkley's efforts was the King of Kings Missionary Movement. Joseph N. Hibbert founded the Ethiopian Coptic Faith and Leonard P. Howell[1], the most dynamic of the three, established the first Rastafarian Community (known as Pinnacle) in Jamaica.

Each group provided social, cultural and spiritual support for its members. In recent times religious worship in some groups has been along the lines of the Ethiopian Orthodox Church and a large portion of the Movement are baptised members of the Church. Most Rastafarians organised amongst themselves in their respective communities and all have their allegiance to one of the four major organisations that now exists. They are as follows:

(1) Black International Congress Church of Salvation

Known within the Rasta Community as "Bobo Shanti", this organ was led by the late Prince Emmanuel Edwards, an elder Rastafarian who organised the first Rasta convention in Jamaica in 1958. Today this organ is still run along the lines of Howell's Pinnacle Camp. They implement and maintain a rigid secular church order. However, they have demonstrated openly in public on issues they see relevant to their struggle, for example, President Reagan's visit to Jamaica in 1982.

Footnote: 1: More research has shown that Leonard P. Howell was also a member of the EWF Inc.

This group of Brethren are identifiable by their distinctive head wrap, which they wear to cover their locks. They have also developed a viable economy in Jamaica selling brooms all over the island. They were represented in Ethiopia in the Centenary year. Ninety percent of the membership reside in Jamaica, but they also have community in Ghana, West Africa and Ethiopia.

(2) The Twelve Tribes of Israel Organisation

This group was first known as Charter 15 of the Ethiopian World Federation, Inc. in Jamaica, but was dissolved in 1973 and is now known as Twelve Tribes of Israel. They have a large membership in Jamaica, England and the U.S.A. Their leader is called Prophet Gad and they adopt their names according to the month of the year, April to March, in which each member is born. These names follow those of the Twelve Tribes of Israel in the Old Testament, i.e. Reuben, Simeon, Levi, Judah, Issachar, Zebulun, Dan, Gad, Asher, Napthali, Joseph and Benjamin.

One of their main contributions has been the development of a strong cultural and disciplined atmosphere at their dance functions, which attract large followings of Brethren and Sistren. They have also some leading reggae artists as members of their organ. Twelve Tribes are also the most liberal within the Rastafarian Community. Some of their members now reside on the Land in Ethiopia, and in Ghana. They were represented on the Centenary trod to Ethiopia.

(3) Jah Rastafari Ivine Theocratic Government

This group, known as the Nyahbinghi House, represents the oldest and the largest segment of the Rastafarian community. It is governed by a council called "The Issemble of Elders". As yet they have not developed any formal constitution and by-laws, as, for example, the Ethiopian World Federation, Inc. However, the Binghi house base their operation on the Bible.

The Nyahbinghi House attends gatherings which are called Binghi or Nyahbingi. This involves drumming, chanting and reasoning on various issues concerning the Movement. The sacred herbs (marijuana) is used during these sessions, which can last between 3 days to a month in Jamaica, and is held on the hills in different parts of the island. In England these sessions are held on one night only, due to the different environment. The Nyahbingi House is seen within the Rastafari Movement as the guardian of the Higher Principles of Rastafari and enjoys the support of the majority of the Rastafarian community in Jamaica, U.S.A., England, and the Caribbean. They were represented on the Centenary visit to Ethiopia.

(4) The Ethiopian World Federation, Inc.

This organisation was established through the authority of H.I.M. Emperor Haile Selassie I in 1937 in America by Dr Malaku E. Bayen (see background history). In its early history this organisation served as a pressure group during the Ethio-Italian war 1936-41. After the war His Majesty granted 500 acres of land in Ethiopia through the Federation. The Ethiopian World Federation Inc. first came to Jamaica in 1938, and both Joseph N. Hibbert and Archibald Dunkley and their followers were foundation members of this Local (E.W.F Inc. Local 17).[1] Since then many members of the Rastafarian Community have embraced this organ, most notably from the Nyahbinghi House. These two groups have always worked very closely.

Footnote: [1]see footnote on page 152

In recent times the E.W.F. Inc. has been very strong in England and have support also in the USA. A significant section of the organ are also baptised members of the E.O.C. This organ has a formal constitution and by-laws. They were well represented on the Centenary visit to Ethiopia.

At present the EWF Inc. is based also in Ethiopia and Ghana where it has land. In Ethiopia they have been registered as a non-governmental organisation (NGO) with NGO status. This is in keeping with the requirements of the various Ethiopian Governmental departments, e.g. the Relief and Rehabilitation Commission (R.R.C.) and the Oromo Education Bureau. Under the NGO status, the organisation is obligated to implement certain developmental projects.

Since 1983 the People of Amamole in Ghana, through the Ministry of National Mobilisation and Agriculture, have also given land to the EWF Inc. Up until now, though, the development on this land has been slow.

On the general level, the organ continues to make strides in international works and involvement. In this regard, the revitalised EWF Inc. held its second International Convention in Shashamane, Ethiopia, thus taking it periodically from the regular HQ venue in New York City.

Diet

Since the early development of the Movement every Brethren and Sistren observed the prohibition in Leviticus chapter 11 verse 3: *"Whatsoever parteth the hoof, and is clovenfooted and cheweth the cud among the beasts, that shall ye eat"*. Verse 9: *"These shall ye eat of all that are in the waters: whatsoever hath fins and scales in the waters, in the seas and in the rivers, them shall ye eat."* Verse 10: *"And all that have not fins and scales in the seas, and in the rivers, of all that move in the waters and of any living thing which is in the waters they shall be an abomination unto you."* Therefore, all Rastafari avoid pork, shell-fish, and creeping animals. Indeed, the ideal is now a special vegetarian / vegan ideal known as 'Ital'[1].

Marijuana (Herbs)

"He causeth the grass to grow for the cattle, and herb for the service of man, that he may bring forth food out of the earth." Psalms 104 verse 14.

The use of marijuana by the Rastafarian Community has brought them into direct confrontation with the establishment and the police. However, Rastafarians believe they are just observing the Bible and practicing their culture by using herbs in their social gathering. It is used in a disciplined way and is not seen as a drug. To members of the Rastafarian Community, drugs are manufactured by multi- national companies and involve the use of chemicals. But a plant which is grown and ripened by the sun and used in a disciplined way is no different from other plants or herbs that are used for cooking. Rastafarians are asking the establishment to legalise marijuana. They believe the law should be changed so that members of the Rastafarian Community are not made criminals for smoking herbs. Rastafarians are God-fearing people, and law abiding. Their only so-called crime against society is smoking marijuana. There are those in society who take advantage of this by adopting the Rastafari look and use the Movement to cover their unlawful activities.

Footnote [1]: Many Brethren and Sistren have stopped eating meat and now live on a vegan diet ('Ital'). Some who are baptised members of the Ethiopian Orthodox Church also observe their fast days.

It is strange that in the capital of Holland, Amsterdam, one can buy marijuana in any coffee shop and smoke it in a civilised way without fear of the police. Yet in other parts of the Western world, the law is still Dickensian and oppressive.

We believe the Rastafarians should be exempt from the charge of smoking herbs, which I and I see as part of our culture, something our ancestors practiced long ago in Africa. Rastafarians are law abiding members of the community in which they live, and their use of herbs as a sacrament should not be used to criminalise them.

21. Mission To Africa Report 1961

The Hon. N. W. Manley Q.C.
Premier of Jamaica
Ministry of Development, Kingston

Dear Premier
The unofficial "Back-to-Africa" Mission to Africa sponsored by your government travelled inside five African States and had talks with the heads of each state about "their migration policies and the possible movement of persons from this island to settle in those countries". The Mission found in all the territories a ready acceptance of the principle of "repatriation of Africans living abroad, to the ancestral land", as it was enunciated by the delegates on the Mission. Since the Mission was not empowered to enter into commitments with these African States, their governments declared their readiness to enter into discussions with your government so as to deal with the mechanics of future migrations. The Mission told the African governments that it did not believe it would be the policy of your government to burden their governments with all the financial requirements of any such migration.

Delegates of the Mission were Messers. Filmore Alveranga, Douglas Mack and Mortimer Planner of the Rastafarian Movement; Mr Westmore Blackwood of the Universal Negro Improvement Association; Dr M.B. Douglas of the Afro-Caribbean League; Mr Cecil George Gordon of the Ethiopian World Federation Inc.; Mr Z. Munroe Scarlett of the Afro-West Indian Welfare League.

Serving as advisors to the Mission were Dr L.C. Leslie, Medical Practitioner who also acted as leader of the Mission; and Mr Victor Reid, Journalist and author.

The Mission found that the skills of such Jamaican artisans as carpenters, masons, mechanics were generally of a higher order than the African, and that there was a shortage of artisans in these States.

The Mission found that food production in most of the countries was (1) low, and/or (2) often lacked variety. All of these countries, although lying in the tropical belt, were still importing sugar, but Ethiopia has a sugar factory turning out over 40,000 tonnes a year. The Mission found a desire, in the territories visited, for three departments of skilled immigrants: a) Professional and Technical, b) Artisans, c) Farmers.

The African hosts to the Mission all observed that persons entering Africa in any migration scheme should do so with the intention of becoming permanent residents in the country, and not as transients. The question of citizenship would present no difficulty, they pointed out, since special arrangements would be made in this connection. But the matter of assimilation would be of prime importance and it was recommended that this be considered for special study on both sides. On almost every occasion it was a point for earnest conversation that centuries of exposure to western ideas and customs must tend to modify Jamaicans (and all the Black people of the western hemisphere) into a way of life dissimilar to the African. Impatience with the African's traditions and customs, or too hard a try to "bring him into line" would wreck the finest efforts of the scheme. It could also operate the other way around.

It was therefore strongly submitted by some members of African Government that an advance "goodwill corps" from both sides, Jamaica and the African States, should be sent into the countries of source and destination, to study and to teach.

Commencing at Ethiopia where we remained for one week, the Mission went, in turn, to Nigeria (2 weeks), Ghana (1 week), Liberia (6 days) Sierra Leone (1 week). Prior to this, on our way from Jamaica, we spent two days in New York and one week in London. Altogether, the Mission was away for 61 days. At all points, the courtesy and welcome was outstanding. In Ethiopia, the Emperor presented each member of the Mission with a gold medal and instructed that all expenses incurred in the country (including hotel bills) be paid by His government. The Abuna (or Arch-bishop) of the Ethiopian Orthodox State Church also received the Mission and presented each member with a complete Ethiopian national costume. The Abuna, in making the presentation said that he did not only give the robes to the Mission as gifts, but that they should all know themselves to be Ethiopians. At Freetown, in Sierra Leone, medals were also presented to the Mission by the Mayor and Council.

In Nigeria, members of the Mission were also each presented with a complete national costume by the Governor General, Dr Nnamdi Azikiwe, and twice was received by him at Government House.

The week that the Mission was in Ghana was also the occasion of the state visit by President Sukarno of Indonesia. However, Dr Kwame Nkrumah nonetheless twice received the Mission, first in the official talks and again as his guest at a private entertainment put on for the Indonesian President.

The Mission was also the dinner guest of the President of Liberia, Mr William V.S. Tubman at his private lodge outside Monrovia after our official talks in his office.

In Sierra Leone, Dr the Hon. Sir Milton Margai, the Prime Minister, also entertained the Mission and a visiting trade

Mission from the United Arab Republic at a reception at the state residence which was attended by his Cabinet, Government Officials, the Diplomatic Corps and prominent persons in the country.

Of particular significance, the Mission considers the enthusiasm with which the African States marked this first serious exertion in a hundred years to activate the Back-to-Africa idea cherished in many countries. The Mission found in Africa, former West Indian, Brazilian, Mexican and American Black nationals whose ancestors had been taken to Brazil, Mexico, the U.S and the West Indies as slaves. The comment from these and from African statesmen was laudatory at the boldness and penetration with which the Jamaican Government had tackled the idea.

One of the problems that should be investigated by the Jamaican Government is the matter of land tenure. An example is in some areas where lands are vested in tribal chiefs. However, in various countries where this situation holds, the Mission was assured that changes in these "native laws and customs" were contemplated so that central governments would have the authority to deal with purchases and so on.

The Mission invited all the Heads of State to visit Jamaica, and the invitations were accepted. The Mission also suggested the exchange of students between all the countries visited and the West Indies and the suggestion was accepted in each instance.

The Report which follows turns on discussions which were held not only with government officials, but also with private citizens.

The Mission is grateful for the opportunity afforded them to take part in this historic event and trusts that the results anticipated will be forthcoming.

Ethiopia

Our first contact with those sections of the continent of Africa towards which the Mission looked for "the possible movement of persons...to settle," was Ethiopia. We arrived there on Sunday April 16th.

We were met at the Addis Ababa airport with every courtesy by officials of the Foreign Ministry led by Ato Getaneh Haile-Mariam, Chief of the English and Commonwealth Department of the Ministry of Foreign Affairs, and were put up at the Ghion Hotel, one of Addis Ababa's finest hotels. Lidj Ayele-Work Abebe, a senior officer of the Ministry, was detailed to looked after the members of the Mission during their stay in Ethiopia.

Slated for us were meetings with the Ministers of Foreign Affairs, the Interior, Commerce and Industry, Agriculture, and National Community Development. At each of these meetings, our reason for visiting Ethiopia were related by the leader of the Mission, Dr. Leslie, and further supplemented by remarks from other delegates. We were give very attentive and obviously sympathetic hearing by the Ministers who assured us that our proposals would receive their active attention. While we awaited the summons from the Emperor, we were enabled by the attention of the government to see as much of the country, its institutions and life as was possible. Accordingly we made visits to such places as the famous Co-operative Farm at Awasa, Her Imperial Majesty's Handicraft and Technical School, the Debre Birhan Community Centre, the Point Four Farm at Gimma, Wonji Sugar Estate; such works as the Koka Dam and to Shashamane, the land the Emperor gave about 10 years ago for people of African origins domiciled outside the continent and who desired to return. Much talk and thinking has been directed to Shashamane by people in the Back-to-Africa movements in Jamaica and we'll discuss it later in the report. The Mission went by air to Gimma to see the coffee plantations there.

We were received by the Emperor in one of His palaces at Addis Ababa on Friday April 21st. He welcomed the members of the Mission as "brothers of one blood and race". The purpose of the Mission was explained by Dr Leslie. In His reply, the Emperor said that Ethiopia would always be open to people of African origin who lived in the West and who desired to return. It had been explained to Him that this was an unofficial Mission, although sponsored by the Jamaican Government, and the Emperor asked that a delegation of experts be sent from Jamaica to discuss the various facets of migration. His Majesty also hoped we would "send the right people". His Majesty also expressed eagerness for an exchange of students and scholars between His country and the West Indies and said He would instruct the Minister of Education to instantly explore the situation.

At the conclusion of the Audience, the members of the Rastafarian group on the delegation presented His Imperial Majesty with the following gifts: (1) a carved wooden map of Africa with a painting of the Emperor done by a Rastafarian Brethren; (2) a number of photographs of Rastafarians and a painting of Navy Island also executed by Rastafarian Brethren; (3) a red, green and gold scarf woven by Mr Planno, one of the delegates and a portrait of His Imperial Majesty in military uniform painted by Mr Sporty Green, a Rastafarian.

The climate of Ethiopia is equable for Jamaicans. Ethiopia lies closer to the equator (5 degrees) than Jamaica (15 degrees) but it is mountainous enough to produce a climate mostly remindful of Mandeville (Jamaica). From Addis Ababa, which is over 8,000 feet above sea level, the land falls away to the warmer coastal areas. Rainfall over the whole huge country is adequate (high: 61"; low: 34.7") and helps to provide the striking agricultural potential that leads an official Ethiopian government release into stating: "There are vast areas of agricultural land which afford ample reserves for future expansion."

The Emperor, after it had been drawn to his attention that our people were skilled in sugar cane cultivation and sugar manufacturing for over 300 years and had also been foremost in its establishment in Cuba, urged the members of the Mission to visit Ethiopia's lone sugar estate and look at the works. Ethiopia, up to a few years ago, imported all its sugar. It still imports a large percentage, but there is a very modern sugar factory at Wonji which makes around 40,000 tonnes a year. Jamaica mills out some half a million tonnes a year.

Of approximately 400,000 square miles in extent, Ethiopia has a population of 22 million people. A point of comparison: Jamaica has one and a half million on 4,000 odd square miles. The West Indies has over 3,000,000 people and 8,000 square miles. Thus the Jamaican population density is some 60 times greater than Ethiopia's.

The Emperor at His Audience told the Mission that "Ethiopia will grow anything, cattle, sunflower (for oil), sugar cane, cotton, bananas, vegetables, coffee, cereal and pulses all throughout the lush countryside. Last count has the cattle population at over 23 million head, sheep number over 22 million and goats over 16 million."

"Coffee originated in Ethiopia and the fine "arabica" type grows so wildly that it forms part of the underbrush in the forests." Varieties are plentiful and coffee beans to over £13 million was exported in 1959. There are now coffee cooperatives functioning. The establishment of other cooperatives is proceeding. Says a government statement: "We could undoubtedly increase coffee production by establishing large organised plantations and by encouraging the people to set up small plantations." The Mission pointed out that Jamaicans were long-time coffee growers and could aid in the expansion of this crop.

Food supplies are relatively cheap and plentiful and provide the working class Ethiopians with a diet that is rich in carbohydrates but said to be short in fats; although by expert accounts, it is adequate in vitamins. At any rate, the medical people queried observed that the nutritional status was good, that there was no malnutrition in the children, and members of the Mission can testify to the tastiness of the Ethiopian "national" dish, the Injera and Watt (Injera is a pancake like soft bread made from a vegetable extract called Ttef; Watt is a meat sauce with red peppers, onions and other spices).

Housing is in short supply and expensive in some categories. Migrants would be encouraged to make full use of the unlimited supply of clay and timber available for building purposes. Indeed, a sturdy example is witnessed at Shashamane, the first or "pilot" settlement attempted by West Indians in Ethiopia. Shashamane, a beautifully rolling country lying between the Malkoda and Shashamane rivers on the lower slopes of the Addis plateau about 160 miles from the city, was years ago designated by the Emperor as a giftland to Black people of the West desiring to settle in Ethiopia. This was confirmed to the Mission by His Imperial Majesty the Emperor Haile Selassie I Himself.

James and Helen Piper were originally from Monserrat. After living in New York for some years, where they were members of The Ethiopian World Federation Inc., they migrated to Ethiopia in 1948. James Piper taught carpentry at the technical school in Addis until 1952 when he returned to New York. A year later he was back in Ethiopia on a decision to take up the offer of lands which had been made through the E.W.F. Inc.

In the company of a small group of West Indians and Afro-Americans, which included a Jamaican girl, Julia Green formerly of Annotto Bay and Dr David Talbot of British Guyana (now Advisor on English publications with the Ethiopian Ministry of Information), they explored the countryside until they came to Shashamane. There they settled, living in a hastily thrown up mud-hut until they had built their present comfortable bungalow. Only the Pipers are still at Shashamane (they are now Ethiopian citizens). They farm scientifically, and also run a corn mill, grinding the neighbourhood corn for a fee. They are happy and prosperous. They own about 50 head of cattle, corn and sunflower fields, and a goat herd. *"The land at Shashamane could take many more families"*, Helen Piper said. *"We would like to see more West Indians here."*

At present there are not many industries in Ethiopia but the country is being geared towards industrialisation. There are canning and button factories, textile factories, a brewery, cigarette, cement, soap and matches factories. Mining is limited but the government operates two gold mines and a platinum mine. Oil is being sought.

Wages permit adequate purchase of basics but little luxuries (example: a chauffeur earns £10-£15 a month; carpenter £20-£25 a month). The Mission believes that the potential for migrants to Ethiopia lies in agriculture. In this field, the potentials are vast. Schools and medical facilities are widening. The language barrier, if it exists is not formidable. English is the lingua franca of the country (indeed, all of West Africa too).

On one point the Mission would like to make an observation. There has been a notion, spread by certain publications and touted by many non-Africans, that people of Ethiopia, and the Emperor, consider themselves above and apart from the people of central Africa, the so-called "negroids". Nothing of the kind has been observed by the Mission on their visit to Africa. The people of Ethiopia live in equality and concord. Said the Emperor at the last meeting of the Independent African States held in Addis Ababa: *"Socially and culturally, we must develop those natural bonds of our people that have been stretched and weakened through the fragmentation of our continent by the colonial practices of divide and rule. We must see to it that the history of each other of our people is known to the others and appreciated throughout the continent."*

A point of interest is that on Friday 21st April, two members of the Mission, Mr Cecil Gordon and Mr Z. Munroe Scarlett were baptised into the Ethiopian Orthodox State Church by His Holiness Abuna Basilios, Primate of Ethiopia, Bishop Theophilus and Paulus, Bishop of Jerusalem. Mr Gordon represents the Ethiopian World Federation Inc. and Mr Scarlett Administrator of the Afro-West Indian Welfare League.

Nigeria

Alhaji Sir Abubakar Tafawa Balewa, Prime Minister of the Federation of Nigeria, was about to leave for Sierra Leone to take part in that country's celebrations of independence, when the Mission arrived in Lagos on 23rd April, but the official welcome was full and friendly. A senior Assistant Secretary in the Ministry of the Interior, Mr Babatunde Harper, was designated to accompany the Mission in its two weeks tour of the Federation and a wide programme of visits was planned. An early call was paid on the Oba (or King of Lagos), at his palace in the city, who declared that West Indians migrating to Nigeria would be welcomed not as immigrants, but as people returning *"to the land of their fathers"*. Calls were also made on the Minister of Labour and Social Welfare, Hon J.A. Johnson and the Minister of State for External Affairs, Senator Dr Esin A. Esin. A high point of the week in Lagos was the meeting with the Governor General Dr. Azikiwe. At each call the purpose of the Mission was explained and the Mission's principle of "repatriation to Africa" was received by the officials with enthusiasm.

Dr Azikiwe, in his speech of welcome at the State House, spoke warmly of the "debt due to West Indian teachers, pastors and settlers by the West African nations". He observed that he himself had been taught by West Indian teachers and states that the philosophies of the late Marcus Garvey were responsible, in large measures, for his work towards the independence of Nigeria. He hoped now that the question of migration would be taken up at the official level.

Dr Esin, the Minister of State for External Affairs, remarked that "the people in the West Indies are more socially advanced than us and that could create a problem", but he hoped that the governments of West Africa and the West Indies, "would address themselves to it". He cited and compared the Back-to-Africa movement with the Jewish restoration to Israel and advanced that Nigeria could "absorb all the three million in the West Indies, without any trouble". The people of African origin in the West, "are bound to come home", said the Minister.

The members of the Mission were again guests of their Excellencies Dr and Mrs Azikiwe later in the week and accompanied them to an evening performance of a touring United States show.

The Nigerian tour allowed for the Mission to make visits to each of the three territories in the Federation.

Western Nigeria

In Ibadan, one of the early calls in the programme, planned for the Mission by the government of the region, was on the Chief Secretary and Head of the Civil Service, Chief Adepo who pledged that the civil service would do all in its power "to promote the Back-to-Africa Movement because the people of the West Indies were African". The Chief Secretary said that in his student years in Britain, he could recall that West Indians there had shown no interest whatever in Africa, but he was gratified that this feeling had now been changed.

The Acting Premier of the region, the Oba C.D. Akran who received the Mission on the day of arrival in Ibadan, expressed his government's interest in the purpose of the Africa visit. The Premier said that the region's lack of skilled personnel was evidenced in the fact that much of the money earmarked for development purposes was unspent, because of the shortage in trained workers. "We would rather recruit the skills from among our brothers abroad," rather than from among European expatriates, the Acting Premier said. A luncheon attended by the officials and prominent residents of Ibadan was given to the Mission on the day of arrival.

Much favourable comments were constantly heard about the performance of West Indians in Nigeria by Nigerian officials (and in the other countries too).There is a fairly strong Jamaican colony in all three regions. At Ibadan, the Mission was given a cocktail party by West Indian residents of the city at the home of the Solicitor General, Mr D.A.R. Alexander and Mrs Alexander. Mr Alexander is a St. Lucian and Mrs Alexander is a Jamaican.

Northern Region

We arrived at the capital Kaduna, in the middle of the final campaigns of the regional elections. The predictable result was that all the ministers were out of office, stumping in the sticks, so to speak, and the regrets of the Premier, Sir Ahmadu Bello, the Sardauna of Sokoto, were conveyed to us by the Deputy Secretary. Meetings were however held with the senior civil servants and the Mission's purpose explained. The quite comprehensive programme included visits to a textile mill, the legislature and to the remarkable Institute of Administration in Zaria, where in-service training was given to civil and municipal officers and their wives.

Eastern Region

At Enugu, calls were made on the Governor and the Premier of the Eastern Region and the Mission's purpose outlined to them. Sir Francis Ibiam, the Governor (a doctor of medicine), gave a luncheon for the Mission and spoke enthusiastically of the possibility of West Indian migration. A dinner was given by the Premier, Dr Michael Okpara who declared that Africans, wherever they were or lived were welcome in a free Nigeria because "if other nations do not want them, Africa needs them and Nigeria is the home of Black Africa. We have the lands they need."

In Enugu, the Mission was contacted by Mr K.O.K. Onyioha, the Provincial Publicity Manager for the region, who stated that he had sent a letter to the Premier of Jamaica making an offer of lands from his clan, the Nkporo Clan in Bende Division, to any Jamaicans of African descent who desired to return. It could take you five years of residence to become a citizen of Nigeria, but the government reserves the right to confer it at any time; instantly if it wishes.

Forty million Nigerians occupy the country's over 370,000 square miles that is divided into three regions by the Y-flow of the Niger. Lagos,* the federal capital on an island at the confluence, is a humming modern city bustling with a quarter million people who trade in its innumerable small and large businesses (its women small traders, as in Ghana, are famous), work in over 200 industries, including soap factories, breweries, mass producing plant for metal containers, automobile assembly plant, foundries, timber mills, etc. Skilled labour is limited.

A reflection of the salary scales can be seen in the fact that clerk typists in the municipal service commence at 76 p.a. Skilled workers receive about 12/- to 18/- per day. Unskilled commence at 4/6 per day.

Nigeria's three regions provide for important differences in the ownership of land. In the predominantly agricultural country, this must have a profound effect on immigrants with an eye on farming. In the eastern and western regions, land may be bought and sold. In the northern region, the land is vested in the government, but a change in this system is contemplated by the federal government.

Western Nigeria has six and a half million people. Sixty percent of its small workers are farmers. Western-type foods are as expensive as imported foods in Jamaica, but native food is plentiful and reasonably priced within the economy. Some local foods are corn-porridge taken with eggs, or hard boiled eggs and spring onions (for breakfast); pounded yam or garri with vegetable-meat soup (for lunch); a thick porridge with fish or chicken stew and fried plantain (for dinner).

Western Nigeria has the greatest variety of export crops in the federation. Among them are cocoa, palm oil and kernels,

*Footnote: Nigeria's capital is now Abuja (Editor)

cotton, timber, rubber and kola nuts. A government marketing agency handles the export crops.

A point worthy of mention is the large and efficient rehousing scheme in progress by the Federal Government. The Lagos Executive Development Board has evacuated 10,000 slum dwellers into new houses at Surulere alone. On one housing estate for low-bracket earners, rental is fixed at 16/6 per room per month.

Eastern Nigeria has nearly 8 Million people on twenty - nine and a half thousand square miles which makes it almost twice as thickly populated as the Western region. The industrial and agricultural pattern is like the Western region. Its contact with the Caribbean is pronounced, particularly through teachers and missionaries; the name "Calabar" and its associations is too well known in Jamaica to need further comment.

Northern Nigeria is the giant among the regions, taking some 18 million people on its more than 250,000 square miles. In this fantastically "empty" country that is roughly just about self supporting in agriculture, one worker in the statistics, produces enough food to feed himself and almost "two other people"; that is, all the "too olds" and the children. The agricultural worker in Britain and the U.S. produces enough to feed 15 persons, five times the quantity produced in northern Nigeria. At the present rate, it seems that none of the agricultural workers could be released into industry. Manpower and efficiency is needed.

But industry is already storming into the northern region. In the old walled city of Kano, factories are producing cloth, tinned meats, shoes, processing rubber, palm oil, making iron beds, sweets etc. In talks to the Mission, statesmen in the east and west thought thousands of West

Indian workers could be accommodated in the north. Needed would be a change in the law to provide for easier land tenure. We understand that the federal government is exploring this.

Ghana

The Mission arrived in Ghana on Monday May 8th, and was received by Dr Nkrumah two days later. He asked that the Mission be presented to him before meeting any other official.

In Accra, Ghana, we went to President Dr Kwame Nkrumah at Flagstaff House, his residence. The Mission was received in the cabinet room, and Dr Nkrumah said, "How shall I put it? Our meeting is historic. It has historic significance not only because we're blood relations but also because so many attempts were previously made and failed. Marcus Garvey tried but was prevented."

The President also said that he was "happy that there were forces at work in the Caribbean" which were responsible for the present Mission. He expressed his agreement with the Back-to-Africa movement and paid tribute to Marcus Garvey who had been his "inspiration". He said the Back-to-Africa desire had to be realistically approached. The two people, West Indians and Africans, had developed separately over the intervening years when they were apart. There would have to be adjustments.

Dr Nkrumah asked for a copy of the Garvey bust as well as any photographs of it. He said he wanted to visit the West Indies "to see his brothers and sisters there". He recalled that he had been taught by Jamaican teachers, and asked to be remembered to Dr Ivan Lloyd.

After the outlining of our purpose by Dr Leslie, Dr Nkrumah said that he would appoint a special committee to talk with the Mission and accordingly, five officials named by the President met the Mission on Thursday 11th May. The Committee was headed by Mr Tawia Adamafio, Minister of State for Presidential Affairs, and included Miss Nana Kobina Nketsia, Cultural Advisor to the Government, Sir Tsibu Darku, Chairman of the Cocoa Marketing Board, Mr M.F. Dei Anang, Secretary-General, Ministry of Foreign Affairs and Mr E.N. Okoh, Deputy Secretary to the Cabinet. The Committee enquired about the number of persons who desired to return to Africa and was informed that while they numbered "many thousands", there was no accurate information on this point. The matter of skills was discussed and delegates of the organisations represented on the Mission explained the varying degree of skills which were possessed by their members.

It was pointed out as an example that the seven Jamaican delegates presented included a mechanic fitter (Mr Mack), a shoemaker-farmer (Mr Alveranga), a weaver (Mr Planno), all three being Rastafarian, a potter (Mr Blackwood, U.N.I.A.), a port worker (Mr Gordon, Ethiopian World Federation Inc.), a chiropractor (Mr Scarlett, Afro-West Indian Welfare League) and a dental surgeon (Dr Douglas, Afro-Caribbean League). Delegates informed the Committee that other skills were possessed by most of their members and stressed that economic farming on small acreages was a way of life in the Jamaican rural community.

After further discussion, the Committee suggested that on our return a memorandum of the number and categories of people desirous of migrating to Ghana should be sent them as early as possible. Both peoples, Jamaicans and Ghanians, would have to be educated into understanding each other. Ghana was the first of the former British colonies to receive independence (1957) and is well on their economic drive. Going into operation this month is a plan to recruit every unemployed person who can read and write, to be trained as teachers. The official goal is full literacy within ten years.

Ghana mines gold, manganese, diamonds, bauxite, but agriculture is the mainstay of its economy with cocoa far and away its most valuable crop. It is the most prosperous of African states, exceeded only by the Union of South Africa in income per capita. Its wealth comes mostly from the Ghana owned and operated cocoa industry. Only citizens of Ghana may own land in the country. Although its domestic food production is high, a large volume is imported. Farming for internal consumption is ripe for increase. There is enough land and palm oil is an important crop.

The Republic contains nearly 92,000 square miles and peopled by seven million. About two million are of working age and last year registered unemployment was 7,000 or 0.35 per cent. Wages in Ghana are in the order of 15/- per day for artisans (carpenters, masons, & c), 7/- for unskilled. Native food is inexpensive; European clothing are about the same as Jamaican prices.

In Ghana, as in all the countries visited, housing is still inadequate, but large housing schemes were also present in all countries, mostly in the urban areas. President Nkrumah said that right now, Ghana could employ all the skilled seamen they could get for their increasing merchant fleet. There are twelve ships in Ghana's Black Star Line and President Nkrumah said that by next year, units of the line would be visiting the West Indies.

The Mission had the honour of meeting the oldest chief of Ghana, Nii Amoo Nakwa II, who is 92 and travelled all the way from Kumasi to meet the Mission. The occasion was a cocktail party given by the Ghana Government for the Mission.

Liberia

A door to migrants was years ago left ajar in the constitution of Liberia. In 1955, a law was enacted to authorise the President to make arrangements for the care of immigrants to Liberia.

President Tubman of Liberia, by whom the Mission was received in the presidential offices in Monrovia, reiterated that the policy was not changed. Liberia would welcome persons of African descent and of all skills "including agriculturalist of all fields and types". Every encouragement is given to people who go into farming. The 1955 law is enriched by a provision granting the issuing of free lands to immigrants, plus three months free housing.

After the deputation explained its purpose at the meeting with the President, Mr Tubman recalled his state visit to Jamaica and said that Jamaica was over-populated and needed easement while Liberia was under-populated and needed people. He said that details would necessarily have to be worked out between the governments and that a pilot project might be the best way to begin. He thought that there might be two levels in any migration plans, a level of "colonisation" (or group) living and one of "integration". He favoured both. President Tubman also said that immigrants should have clean police records. The President said that Liberia would be opened to all peoples of African descent whether they were Rastafarians or not.

The President spoke of the contribution Caribbeans have already made to Liberia. Their descendants had achieved high place in government. (The present Foreign Secretary, Mr Grimes, who was present at the meeting with the President is a descendant of Caribbeans). President Tubman mentioned the names of Barnes, Corniffe, building contractors Clifford Brown (deceased) among many

Jamaicans who had contributed much to the country. Finally he said, *"We, in Liberia agree on the principle of immigration into Liberia of our fellow members of the African Race."*

Liberia was founded by an earlier "Back-to-Africa" movement in 1820 when 88 colonists left New York in the ship "Elizabeth". Except for a few, they were Black people. They bought lands from local chiefs, then had to fight to hold it. Now none but those of African descent may become citizens of Liberia, says Article V of the constitution. To encourage immigration and for a special bias to farmers, unmarried settlers receive 10 acres of farm land, plus one town lot, as well as a free gift. Married settlers receive 25 acres and one town lot.

Prior to 1944, the country was closed to foreign investors except the Firestone Rubber Company. A new "open door" policy has now fantastically pushed the country's income from one million dollars annually, to around 30 million dollars. Long-time Jamaican residents there told the Mission that the face of the country has been entirely changed over the past ten years by the new town, roads and buildings.

Jamaican residents there urged on the Mission that Liberia was the "land of opportunity" to hard workers. Jamaicans began trickling into Liberia during the middle and late 1940s. Today they serve in high ranking government posts, run print shops, canning business, are contractors and builders, and even provided the country with its first female diamond prospector.

Liberia's agriculture produces rubber, cocoa, banana, rice, coffee, palm oil and cassava. Its mines give iron, diamonds, gold, lead and graphite. The iron mines at Bomi contains the world's highest grade ore. But there is no sugar, dairy or citrus production of consequence. Sugar is imported and food production is not nearly enough for local demand. There is an agricultural and industrial credit corporation for making loans to farmers and small industrialists.

Liberia has approximately two million people on 43,000 square miles, less than 50 to the square mile (Jamaica has about 400 to the square mile). The official language is English, but there are many native tongues. The currency is the Liberian and American dollar which are at par. House building materials are mostly clay and sand blocks. U.N.E.S.C.O. is conducting extensive research into building materials. A professor at the University in Monrovia said that "if migration from Jamaica did nothing more than grow the food we needed, their presence would have been more than worthwhile". Diamond mining is important in the country and one of the successful miners is a Jamaican girl named Miss Ethelda James, the country's first female miner.

Sierra Leone

Our final call on the African countries was at Sierra Leone, Monday May 21st. The Prime Minister, Sir Milton Margai received the Mission in his office at Freetown, where he was attended by the Parliamentary Secretary for External Affairs and his Permanent Secretary.

The Mission's reasons for visiting Sierra Leone were given and Sir Milton said the principle of repatriation of West Indians, whose ancestors had been forcibly removed from Africa, was accepted. There was no question about the desirability of having them nor of the welcome they would receive, he said. Sierra Leone could use the skills of West Indians.

The Prime Minister however pointed out that Sierra Leone had received its independence less than a month ago

(April 27th) and would be occupied with "putting its house in order" after the transition. He said that the suggestion for migration from the West Indies would nevertheless be considered by his government at a later date.

Talks were also held with the Hon. G. Dixon Thomas, Minister for Social Welfare and the Hon S.T. Navo, acting Minister for External Affairs. The Mission accompanied Mr Thomas to his home village of Regent (one of the "colony" villages founded by freed slaves from the West Indies) and shared in a youth rally with the Minister. The Mission was afterwards entertained by him at his house.

Sir Milton was also host at a reception for the Mission and for a visiting trade delegation from the United Arab Republic.

One piece of unpleasant publicity received by the Mission occurred at Freetown, where a rehash of a news story published in the London Sunday Despatch of April 23rd and subsequently appearing in the Nigerian Daily Express of April 24th under a Reuter's dateline, was taken up by the Sierra Leone Daily Mail. In a widely spun yarn concerning "plans" afoot to "send home bearded Rastafarians in chains" to Africa, the Sierra Leone paper's article may have sparked the statement purporting to be from Dr John Karefa-Smart, the Sierra Leone Minister for External Affairs, which appeared in the Jamaica Gleaner of June 13th. The statement had him saying that his government was "aware of the nature of the West Indian Rastafarian Movement and will be cautious in considering any application for immigration into Sierra Leone."

Sierra Leone partially owed its establishment to Jamaicans - the 18th century rebellious Maroons who stopped their fighting only to be betrayed by the Governor and banished to Nova Scotia in Canada. Decimated by exposure to the harsh climate, they were subsequently sent to Sierra Leone.

The country is about 28,000 square miles with a population around three million. Its productions for export are palm kernels, coffee, cocoa and cassava. Mining for diamonds and iron produces a big slice of its income. Last year they made £19.5 million on mining. Bauxite mining should commence next year.

Its industries included a tobacco factory, nail factory, a brewery and oxyacetylene plant to the east of Freetown. The government plans to increase the agricultural export in Sierra Leone, especially in oil palms. Much food is still imported. Rice is also down for wide-scale planting. "We plan to turn an army of planters loose on the land. We are training our farmers in the use of mechanical implements," an official at the big experimental station at Njala told the Mission. The land at hand is more than ample for twice and three times the population, he said.

A reception was given the Mission by the Mayor, Alderman and Councillors of Freetown, at which medals were presented to the members.

Appendix "A"

Mr Alveranga, one of the Representatives of the Rastafarians reported on a meeting with the Abuna at which the divinity of Haile Selassie I was discussed.
Mr Alveranga says: "Rastafarian members of the Mission discussed with His Holiness the Abuna Basilios, the divinity of the Emperor Haile Selassie I, as the living God, the Returned Messiah, the King of Kings" (Revelations 17). His Holiness said that the Bible was speaking of Christ."

"We, the Rastafarians showed the relation, by biblical proof, that the Emperor Haile Selassie I was the same Christ sitting upon David's throne (Acts 2 verses 29-32). The Abuna said eventually to us that "the Bible could be interpreted that way". All other delegates on the Mission were present L .C Leslie, M.B. Douglas , Cecil G. Gordon, W. Blackwood, V. Reid, Z. Munroe Scarlet, Filmore Alvaranga, Douglas Mack, Mortimo Planno.

The Force That Never Fails - by Marcus Garvey

"The Emperor of Abyssinia will fight not only by Himself, but by the guidance of that divine power and force that never fails. Already He has triumphed in His diplomacy. He stands out as the one diplomat of the world who has been able to convince all races and nations with righteousness of a cause, and to summon them to united action in the preservation of that cause. This is only the first triumph, but it is an indication of the final victory.

Scattered and dispersed, Africa has sent not only her sympathy but her allegiance to the Emperor of Abyssinia, that voice of Africa will never be silenced. It betokens the spirit of new life-the life of a redeemed people. Spontaneously, the Black of scattered Africa, from the United States, the West Indies, South and Central America, Europe and other parts of the Mother Continent went up, not only in supplication, but in avowed determination to see the enemy put down. Mussolini laughs because from his barbaric mind he can see no other glory than that achieved through military prowess. His mighty mechanical forces have been. He has measured the confidence of the mad men that he not only challenges man, but God. "Man has accepted the challenge, God watches over the destinies of men."

No sacrilegious prayer in Rome will save Mussolini and the Italians. No miscarriage of truth will blot out the iniquity of these vile people. Let Abyssinia therefore, go forward with the sword in hand and as Gideon's band became triumphant against the presumptive superior forces of the enemy, so shall Haile Selassie lead Ethiopia back to her glory and inspire the Black man to the hope of once more worshipping under his own vine and fig tree."

(Marcus Garvey: The Black Man Vol.1 N.2. 1935)

22. Chronology of the Movement

14th c. BC (1300 BC)
Moses takes an Ethiopian wife, Zipporah (Exodus 2:21).

10 th c. BC (900 BC)
Makeda Queen of Sheba visits Solomon and conceives a son, Menelik I. He was subsequently anointed King of Ethiopia by Solomon.

4 th c. AD (300AD)
Ethiopian conversion to Christianity through King Ezana.

1150
Zague Dynasty of Ethiopia came to power, claiming descent from Moses and his Ethiopian wife, Zipporah.

1270
Zague Dynasty ejected, Solomonic Dynasty re-established by Emperor Yekuno Amlak.

1559
Emperor Meenas outlawed Roman Catholicism for Ethiopians.

1565
Queen Elizabeth I gave John Hawkins a Royal Charter and a ship the SS Jesus of Lubeck to transport slaves from Africa to the West Indies.

1885
The Berlin Conference of Europeans planned the invasion and partitioning of Africa among themselves.

1896
Italian invaders defeated by Emperor Menelik II at the Battle of Adowa (Ethiopia).

1914
Marcus Garvey founded the U.N.I.A. and the African Communities League.

1927
Marcus Garvey told the Black people to "Look to Africa when a Black King shall be crowned, for the day of deliverance is near."

1930
November 2nd: Ras Tafari Makonnen was crowned Emperor Haile Selassie I, the 225th Monarch of the Solomonic Dynasty. Birth of the Rastafari Movement. Founding Fathers: Leonard P. Howell, Joseph Nathaniel Hibbert and Archibald Dunkley.

1932
Hibbert and Howell attempt to centralise as one, under the banner of The Ethiopian Coptic Faith, with rules and procedures. Unsuccessful.

1933
Paul Earlington and Vernal Davis along with other Brethren based in Kingston Dungle, through the influence of Robert Hinds, Howell's deputy, recognised Haile Selassie I as the living God. Social reform and migration to Africa was emphasised by this group.

1934
L. P. Howell and his deputy R. Hinds charged for uttering seditious speech against the U.K. and the Jamaican Government. Both were sent to prison; Howell, two years, Hinds, one year. A. Dunkly was also arrested and charged for disorderly conduct. Gaol 30 days.

1935
A. Dunkley placed in mental asylum for five months and twenty one days. J.N. Hibbert was also arrested on three occasions, each time being fined (30/-) thirty shillings.

1935
Italy again invades Ethiopia.

1937
Establishment of the Ethiopian World Federation, Inc. in New York by Dr. Malaku E. Bayen, through the authority of His Imperial Majesty Emperor Haile Selassie I, as the international arm of Ethiopian resistance to the Italian invasion.

1938
Establishment of the Ethiopian World Federation, Inc. in Jamaica. This was local 17. L. C. Mantle was President, Paul Earlington, the Vice President, J.N. Hibbert and A. Dunkley were founder members.

1941
Police raid Howell's "Pinnacle" community. 70 Rastafari Brethren were arrested; 28 of these were sent to prison. Howell also convicted and sent to Spanish Town Prison for two years.

1941
HIM Haile Selassie I re-enters the Ethiopian capital, in victory over Italian aggression (May 5th).

1942
Second local of the Ethiopian World Federation, Inc. was established. This was Local 31. First President William Powell. Leadership disputed and went to Mr Cecil G. Gordon.

1942
HYBF (House of the Youth Black Faith) developed the Nyahbinghi drumming out of the burru drums.

1953
First study of the Rastafari Movement by Professor George Simpson.

1954
Police invaded Pinnacle and jailed many of Howell's followers. Others scattered to other parts of the country. Number of dreadlocks increased in Kingston, and the final break-up of Pinnacle.

1955
Mrs Maymie Richardson came to Jamaica on behalf of the headquarters of the Ethiopian World Federation, Inc. and eleven more locals were established. These were Locals 27, 11, 37, 32, 19, 33 , 40, 41, 43, 7 and 77.

1956
Mr Cecil G. Gordon of Local 19 visited the United States for the 17th annual convention of the E.W.F Inc. Returned as Second International Vice President.

1958
The first Rasta convention called by Prince Emmanuel C. Edwards, lasted 21 days. This group now known as Bobo Shanti.

1959
The emergence of the Rev. Claudius Henry, R.B. and his aborted repatriation scheme. He established an organisation called "The Seventh Emmanuel Brethren". He was charged for sedition and treason and jailed for 10 years.

1959
Riot between Rastafari Brethren and police at Coronation Market in Kingston, Ja. Fifty seven Rastafari Brethren were arrested, many were forcibly shaved.

1959
First convention of the Ethiopian World Federation Inc. in Kingston, Ja. at Davis Lane; lasted four days.

1960
Official Report on the Rastafari Movement by the

University College of the West Indies (U.C.W.I.). This outlined history, doctrine and 10 recommendations. Landmark in Rasta history.

1960
Rastafarians in London had first official meeting with official at the Ethiopian Embassy. This group was a sub-local of Local 37 (E.W.F Inc.) and was named by the imperial Ethiopian Government, "The Jamaica Working Committee".

1961
The Government of Jamaica sponsored Mission to Africa. Representatives from the Ethiopian World Federation, Inc., The Rastafarian Movement, the Universal Negro Improvement Association, The West Indian Welfare League and the Afro-Caribbean League, visited five African states. They were, Ethiopia, Nigeria, Ghana, Liberia and Sierra Leone. Ras Sam Brown campaigned as an independent candidate in the general election, in an organ called "Black Man Party".

1961
The Mission to Africa delegation meet members of the "Jamaica Working Committee" in London. This group in London was to form the "Peoples Democratic Movement", political wing of the Rastafari Movement.

1962
Jamaica gained Independence from Britain.

1963
The emergence of the Organisation of African Unity (O.A.U) in Addis Ababa, endorsed by H.I.M.

1963
The Coral Garden, Holy Thursday, killings blamed on Rasta, resulting in a revengeful brutalisation of members of the

Movement. After the Prime Minister's order to bring in all Rastas dead or alive, the J.B.C. removed Rasta programme "Lion of Judah Time" from the radio.

1966
The visit of His Majestic Emperor Haile Selassie I to Jamaica (April 21-23) and the Caribbean. In July 1966, the Government of Jamaica ordered the police to destroy Back-O-Wall (Rasta commune), bulldozing Rastafarian houses. It was called "Operation Shanty-Town".

1969
The Universal Black Peoples Improvement Organisation (U.B.I.O) was established in London. This organ helped to develop the Rasta Movement in England.

1970
The Ethiopian Orthodox Church was officially established in Jamaica by Abba Mandefro, Head Administrator of the E.O.C.

1971
The Peoples Democratic Movement (political wing of the Rastafarian Movement) based in London, was revitalised briefly.

1972
The Ethiopian World Federation Inc. was officially established in London (Emperor Yohannes Local 33).

1973
His Holiness Abuna Theophilos, Patriarch of the Ethiopian Orthodox Church, visited New York (U.S.A) and then Jamaica. Laid the corner stone of the E.O.C. building. Members of the E.W.F. Inc in London were present on this occasion.

1973
Rasta delegation from London met a group called "Charter 15" (later known as the Twelve Tribes of Israel). They have been functioning from 1968.

1974
The Ethiopian Orthodox Church was officially established in London.

1974
Twelve Tribe of Isreal organisation emerged in Jamaica and later in England.

1975
The overthrow of the Imperial Ethiopian Government. HIM disappears from common view.

1978
Jamaica - Peace Treaty uniting rival political gangs in Kingston. This was acknowledged by the Rastafarian Community.

1978
Rasta convention/groundation held at Heroes Park, Kingston, Ja. Lasted 30 days and resulting in Government forcibly evicting Rastas Jah Lloyd and Ras Makonnen from the park after they called on the cabinet of the Jamaica Government to resign.

1979
Jamaica - Jah Lloyd and Ras Makonnen cut down the British flag at the British High Commission, protesting against British slavery, colonialism, capitalism and imperial domination over Black people.

1980
Stephen McDonald, a Rastafarian, contested a seat in the general election in Jamaica as an independent candidate.

1981
Second Rasta Conference in England, held at Brixton Town Hall, London. Call for unity under the EWF Inc. Groups attended: Rasta International, Tree of Life, Mind Soul and Body, Local 33, Rasta Unity, and R.U.Z. All groups accepted to work under the umbrella of the EWF Inc.

1982
Second Annual Rastafari International Theocratic Conference, held at University College of the West Indies.

1983
Ascento Foxe breaks away from Ethiopian World Federation Inc. and establish Imperial Ethiopian World Federation (I.E.W.F.) Inc. Later went on to establish Church of Haile Selassie I .

1984
Ras Sam Brown came to London as a guest of RUZ President, Jah Bones.

1986
"Rastafari Focus" First International Rasta gathering in England. Organised by R.A.S.

1992
"Year of the Creator". Hundreds of Rastafarians made the historic trip to Ethiopian to celebrate the Centenary of H.I.M Haile Selassie I.

1994
International Rasta gathering in Miami Florida by I.C.O.M.R.A.S. This helped to inspire the Rastafari Economic Development Directory known as R.E.D.D. Also Nelson Mandela was elected President Elect in South Africa.

1995
The 57th Annual Convention of the Ethiopian World Federation, Inc. Brooklyn, NY, 10th-18th July. Its first Convention in 37 years.

1996
Brethren from the Nyahbinghi House in Jamaica and London visit South Africa.

BIBLIOGRAPHY

HAILE SELASSIE I - SILVER JUBILEE
David Talbot

AUTOBIOGRAPHY OF H.I.M HAILE SELASSIE I

CARIBBEAN TIMES
7th August 1981 - 21st November 1986

TIME OUT
24th January - February 7th 1971

WEST INDIAN WORLD
6th-12th August 1976

SOUTH LONDON PRESS
24th September 1976

RASTAFARIAN CRY (1971) Vol.1

THE ETHIOPIAN ORTHODOX TEWAHEDO CHURCH AND ITS ACTIVITIES IN THE WEST
Abba L. Mandefro.

RASTAFARIANS IN GREATER LONDON
(Greater London Council Report)
Report back on consultation (1984)

CATHOLIC MISSION FOR RACIAL JUSTICE: RASTAFARIANS IN JAMAICA AND BRITAIN
Notes and Reports No. 10 January 1982

DREAD: THE RASTAFARIANS OF JAMAICA
Joseph Owen (1979)

REPORT OF THE RASTAFARI MOVEMENT,
Kingston, Jamaica: University College of the West Indies, Institute of Social and Economic Research (1960). Rex Nettleford, M.G. Smith and Roy Augier.

MALUKU E. BAYEN; ETHIOPIAN EMISSARY
TO BLACK AMERICA 1936 - 1941
by William R. Scott.

THE BLACK MAN
Marcus Garvey Vol. 11 December 1935.

PHILOSOPHY AND OPINIONS OF MARCUS GARVEY

FOCUS ON RASTAFARI
A report by Rastafari Advisory Service (R.A.S.) 1988.

RASTA AND RESISTANCE
From Marcus Garvey to Walter Rodney
Horace Campbell 1985

SEX AND RACE Vol.1
J.A. Rogers

NATURE KNOWS NO COLOUR LINE
J.A Rogers

FALSE MESSIAH
Derek Humphrey

JAMAICA : THE SEARCH FOR AN IDENTITY
Katrina Norris 1966

FIGHTING MAROONS OF JAMAICA

RASTAMAN: THE RASTAFARIAN MOVEMENT IN ENGLAND (1979).
Ernest Cashmore.

KEBRA NEGAST

THE HOLY BIBLE

SOME RASTAFARI WORD TRANSLATIONS

BABYLON
Places and people of downpression and wickedness

BRETHREN / BREDREN
A fellow Rastaman

DAWTA / DAUGHTER
Referring to a woman

DOWNPRESSION
Oppression

EARTHDAY
Birthday

HOLA
Holy

I AND I / INI
Us, our, or we within Rastafari

ITAL
Pure, natural, total, vital

IVINE
divine

JAH
God

LIVITY
Way of life, culture, purpose in life

RAS
Head, title for a Rastafari

RAS TAFARI:
Head Creator, first name of Haile Selassie I, after whom Iand I are called

ZION
Heaven; African homeland